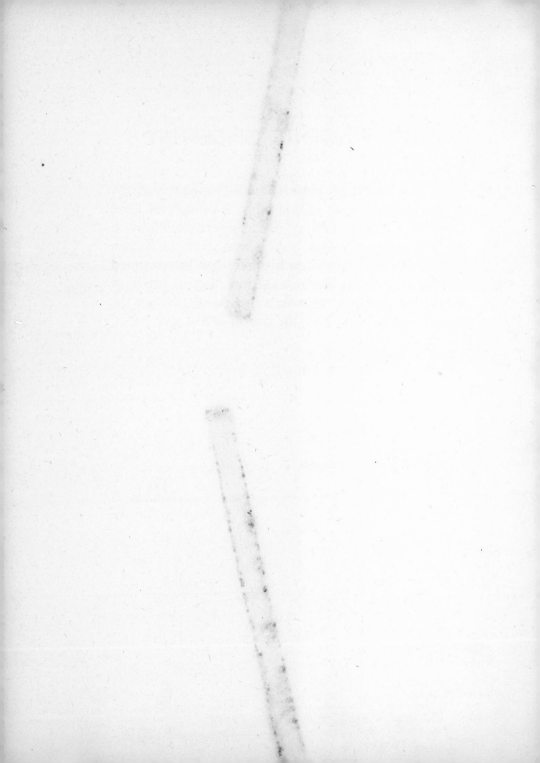

VICE-PRESIDENTS OF DESTINY

Eight Vice-Presidents have succeeded to the Presidency as the result of death in that office. All eight of these "Vice-Presidents of destiny" faced severe challenges in the White House. This book shows how each man met the challenges and how his preceding life prepared him for his role. It also reveals how the conception of the Vice-Presidency influenced the choice of man, the turn of events—and even the course of history.

In Case of the Removal of the President from Office, or of his Death, Resignation, or Inability to discharge the Powers and Duties of the said Office, the Same shall devolve on the Vice-President. . . .

THE CONSTITUTION OF
THE UNITED STATES

Article II, Section 1

Vice-Presidents of Destiny

by
Joseph A. Alvarez

 G. P. PUTNAM'S SONS, NEW YORK

TO MY WIFE

She made it all possible

Contents

PROLOGUE

On Friday morning, November 22, 1963, two red and white jets, Air Force One *and* Air Force Two, *touched down at Love Field, Dallas, Texas. They carried the President and Vice-President of the United States, who never fly together to prevent a single accident from taking both their lives.*

From the airport, the two men, riding in separate limousines, set out for the Dallas Trade Mart, where President Kennedy was scheduled to speak. They never got there. As they neared their destination, the waving, smiling President was cut down by rifle fire. The presidential motorcade raced to Parkland Memorial Hospital. A team of doctors worked feverishly to save the young President's life. But his condition was hopeless, and at 1:00 P.M., after he had received the last rites of his church, the President was pronounced dead.

Ninety-eight minutes later, on board Air Force One, *Vice-President Lyndon B. Johnson, in accordance with Article II, Section 1 of the Constitution, took the oath as the 36th President of the United States. He was the eighth Vice-President to succeed to the presidency upon death in that office. The first succession, 122 years before, had been quite different.*

I am the President, and I shall be held responsible for my administration. I shall be pleased to avail myself of your counsel and advice. But I can never consent to being dictated to as to what I shall or shall not do.

—JOHN TYLER to his Cabinet upon his succession to the presidency

1 John Tyler: 1841

At sunrise on April 5, 1841, two horsemen rode swiftly into Williamsburg, Virginia, after an all-night journey from Washington. They tethered their mounts in front of a tree-shaded, white colonial house, crossed its large front lawn, and knocked loudly on the front door.

Upstairs, Vice-President John Tyler was awakened by the pounding. He rolled out of bed and, in his nightshirt and nightcap, groped his way downstairs in the thinning darkness. Waiting for him at the door were an officer of the Senate and the Chief Clerk of the State Department, Fletcher Webster, son of the gifted orator Daniel Webster, then Secretary of State. They had come to tell the Vice-President that "by act of God" he was now the 10th President of the United States. The 9th President, William Henry Harrison, had just died of pneumonia, after only a month in office.

Tyler was shocked. No one had bothered to inform him of the President's grave illness, although Harrison's condition had been serious for more than a week. But that was the measure of regard for the vice-presidency. "The most insignificant office that ever the invention of man contrived," John Adams had called it. His successor, Thomas Jefferson, thought little more of the job. "It will give me philosophical evenings in winter," he had quipped, "and rural days in summer."

That is what most Americans thought of the vice-presidency—when they thought of it at all. Tyler himself had returned to Williamsburg from Washington shortly after the inauguration, expecting to divide the next four years between social diversions in Williamsburg and presiding over the United States Senate.

But now General Harrison, war hero of the Battle of Tippecanoe and a dozen other frontier engagements, was dead of pneumonia. And John Tyler, slaveholding southern gentleman and firm states' rights advocate, had inherited the presidential mantle. Tyler asked the details of Harrison's illness. It appeared that the General had talked himself to death. His inaugural address had droned on for two hours—a record—on a cold March day. The sixty-eight-year-old Harrison, neglecting to wear an overcoat, had suffered from exposure. He caught cold which, in his weakened condition, quickly developed into a fatal pneumonia.

Tyler woke the rest of the household and told them the news. Together they ate a hasty breakfast; then the new President left for Washington with the two messengers and his two oldest sons, Robert, twenty-five, and John, twenty-two. By five that afternoon they reached Richmond, where they boarded a special train for the capital.

Twelve hours more of travel lay before Tyler. He had time to think about the awesome responsibilities awaiting him in Washington. There was plenty to think about. The issue of slavery divided North and South, and the question of the national bank split merchant and farmer. In the northeast, England and America were disputing the Maine-New Brunswick border, and in the west, the territory of Texas was charting a course as an independent nation, making ominous European alliances. Worst of all, Tyler's own Whig Party was violently divided on almost all these issues.

The Whig Party was hardly a party at all. Northern Whigs, led by former National Republicans Henry Clay and Daniel Webster, favored high tariffs to protect domestic industry, a national bank to stabilize the currency, federally financed roads and canals and liberal interpretation of the Constitution; and they opposed slavery. Southern Whigs like Tyler and the extremist John C. Calhoun opposed high tariffs, a national bank and federal financing of internal improvements; they believed in slavery, states' rights and strict interpretation of the Constitution. What held them all together was their common hatred of Andrew Jackson and popular democracy.

By 1840 Jackson's successor, Martin Van Buren of Kinderhook, New York, had inherited the Whigs' animosity. Van Buren was seeking a second term as

President. His first term had not been a notable success. The country had been in a severe economic depression since 1837. Unemployment was up, farm prices were down, state banks were failing and the national debt was rising. These conditions naturally favored the party out of power, the Whigs. To win in 1840, they had only to avoid alienating the voters; discontent would do the rest. So the Whigs, not wishing to rock the boat, even though it was sinking, nominated for President General Harrison, a retired war hero who stood for nothing and so might be acceptable to everyone.

"Let him say not one single word about his principles or his creed—let him say nothing—promise nothing," Harrison's campaign manager had advised Whig leaders in an earlier campaign. "Let no committee, no convention, no town meeting ever extract from him a single word about what he thinks now or will do hereafter." Henry Clay agreed. "It is a safe general rule that it is best to remain silent," he said.

Tyler, who had supported Clay for the presidential nomination, was selected as Harrison's running mate to strengthen the appeal of the ticket in the South. "The nomination given to me was neither solicited nor expected," Tyler said. Indeed, it might be said to have come to him by default. It was offered to two or three others first, but no one wanted what was considered a dead-end job.

The campaign itself was marked by distortion, defamation and hokum. When it was over, "Tippecanoe and Tyler too"—perhaps the most effective American political slogan ever coined—had carried the day. Van Buren ("Van, Van is a used-up man") complained ruefully that he had been "lied down, drunk down and sung down."

And now "Tyler too" was ready to pick up the reins of government. Few men, before or since, came to the office with more experience in government. Tyler was fifty-one years old—the youngest President up to that time—and 25 of these years had been spent in public office. He had been a Virginia legislator and governor, a U.S. Congressman and Senator. His Washington experience dated back to 1816, when cows and pigs still slogged through the capital's muddy lanes.

Almost all of Tyler's government experience, however, was as a legislator, a job which does not necessarily prepare a man for the presidency. A legislator makes laws; the President must make policies, execute laws, command the armed forces, negotiate treaties, appoint department heads and judges and provide the nation with leadership.

The only executive office Tyler had held which might have prepared him for the presidency was the governorship of Virginia. But the Virginia constitution had made this office subservient to the state legislature. "As a training ground for executive leadership the governorship of Virginia was deficient in every respect," writes historian Robert Seager II.

Although legislative work does not train a man for the presidency, it seems to whet his appetite for the office. The three great legislators of the day, Clay, Webster and Calhoun, each wanted desperately to be

President. Tyler lacked Clay's flexibility and Webster's and Calhoun's fire. But Jefferson Davis, another colleague, regarded him as "the most felicitous among the orators I have known." And Tyler's dedication to his principles was well known. In 1836 he had resigned from the Senate rather than vote for a resolution that he considered unconstitutional but which the Virginia legislature* had instructed him to support.

This, then, was the man who stepped off the train at Washington on Tuesday morning, April 6th, at 5 A.M. He was slender, almost gaunt, and his long face was dominated by high cheekbones and a prominent Roman nose. His thin lips were set in a firm line, and his silken brown hair, swept back from his high forehead, reached to his coat collar.

Very little is known about his childhood. He was born on March 29, 1790, when Washington was President and the city which bears his name was still on the drawing boards. His boyhood was spent in a "genteel, well furnished dwelling" at Greenway, the Tylers' 1,200-acre plantation in Charles City County, Virginia. When he was seven, his mother died, and he was raised by his father, Judge John Tyler, a close friend of Thomas Jefferson. Judge Tyler believed in slavery, the South and states' rights, and his son absorbed these attitudes intact. Now John Tyler, a gentleman by birth and a Southerner by conviction, was President by accident. Or was he?

The capital was buzzing with confusion. Harrison

---

*Until 1913, when the 17th Amendment provided for their direct election, U.S. Senators were chosen by the state legislatures and were expected to follow their directives.

was the first President to die in office, and nobody was quite sure what Tyler's status was. Henry Clay referred to his fellow Whig as "Vice-President" and predicted his administration would be a regency—a temporary, caretaker government. The members of Harrison's Cabinet regarded Tyler as "acting President." They had addressed the official notice of Harrison's death to "John Tyler, Vice-President of the United States." Former President John Quincy Adams—another Whig —thought Tyler should be designated "Vice-President acting as President."

Americans looked to the Constitution for guidance, but in the area of the presidential succession it was* vague. Article II, Section 1 reads: "In Case of the Removal of the President from Office, or of his Death, Resignation or Inability to discharge the Powers and Duties of the said Office, the same shall devolve on the Vice-President. . . ." The question was to what did "the same" refer? If it referred to "Powers and Duties," the Vice-President became only an acting President; if it referred to "the said Office," he assumed the presidency itself.

Tyler decided "the same" referred to "the Office," and he prepared to assume the full powers and privileges of the presidency. It was a momentous decision, for the issue involved more than a question of grammar and semantics. The holder of the *office* of President inherits not only executive power but vast moral and

---

*The 25th Amendment, ratified February 10, 1967, resolves this vagueness in Section 1: "In case of the removal of the President from office or his death or resignation, the Vice President shall become President."

political powers which a mere acting President cannot effectively exercise. These powers—powers of persuasion, really—are the true powers of the presidency. "I sit here all day trying to persuade people to do the things they ought to have sense enough to do without my persuading them," said Harry S. Truman, who succeeded to the presidency 104 years after Tyler did. "That's all the powers of the President amount to."

Tyler knew that, in the absence of precedent, *he* was setting a precedent; that his decision would have far-reaching consequences. "I am under Providence made the instrument of a new test which is for the first time to be applied to our institutions," he wrote to a friend.

No one could say absolutely what the original framers of the Constitution had intended with respect to the presidential succession; James Madison, the last surviving Founding Father, had died in 1836. Even the clues were inconclusive. The original provision for the presidential succession, drafted in 1787 by the Committee of Detail of the Constitutional Convention, read: "In Case of his [the President's] Removal as aforesaid, Death, Resignation, or Disability to discharge the Powers and Duties of his Office, the President of the Senate shall exercise those Powers and Duties, until another President of the United States be chosen. . . ." This was quite clear: the Vice-President would only "exercise" the "Powers and Duties," not the office, of the presidency. But the Committee of the States and the Committee on Style had recast this draft into its present form, leaving the whole question ambiguous.

The Founding Fathers probably didn't care enough about the vice-presidency to clarify the succession clause. "Such an officer as Vice-President was not wanted," wrote North Carolina's Hugh Williamson, ten days before he signed the Constitution. "He was introduced merely for the sake of a valuable mode of election. . . ."

The point, if it ever was brought to Tyler's attention, made no impression upon him. He refused to be swayed by those politicians—so many of them fellow Whigs—who argued against his assuming the full powers and privileges of the presidency. He did not think it necessary even to take a separate oath as the 10th President. The oath he had taken as Vice-President pledged him to "support the Constitution of the United States"; that, he reasoned, met the requirements of the present situation. Friends, however, persuaded Tyler to take the presidential oath anyway, as an additional "caution." They pointed out to him that the Constitution expressly states that, "Before he enter on the Execution of his Office," the President shall take the presidential oath. So arrangements were made to administer the oath of office as soon as possible.

Meanwhile, the confusion continued, as Americans sought to fathom the constitutional intentions of the Founding Fathers. Oddly enough, the strongest argument for a limited succession seems not to have been used. It is contained in the 12th Amendment (which, presumably, met with the approval of those Founding Fathers still alive in 1804). Referring to a presidential election deadlock which the House of Representatives might not resolve, the amendment states that "the Vice-President shall *act* as President, *as in the case of the death or other Constitutional disability of the President.*" (Italics added.)

Actually, the interpretation of the Constitution depends upon who reads it and how persuasive are his arguments. The Constitution always has been subject to conservative and liberal interpretation, or "strict" and "loose" construction. "A strict constructionist," wrote John Quincy Adams, "would doubt whether the Vice-President has the right to occupy the President's house, or to claim his salary, without an Act of Congress." But John Tyler, a notoriously strict constructionist, chose to claim not only the house and salary, but the office of President. At noon on April 6th, in the parlor of Brown's Indian Queen Hotel, Tyler took the oath as the 10th President of the United States. It was his first executive act.

Tyler had successfully met the first great challenge of his presidency: assuming the full powers of the office. He set an important precedent. His determination and boldness made it possible for the seven men who followed in his footsteps to maintain the full powers of the executive branch of government even in times of national crisis.

It appears that Tyler exceeded his constitutional authority. But so did Jefferson when he authorized the Louisiana Purchase in 1803. And in both instances the nation was the beneficiary.

The new President immediately attended to his duties. On the same day he took his oath, he met with his Cabinet, six men whom Harrison had appointed principally to appease the various factions of the Whig Party. Tyler decided to retain the Cabinet intact to forestall further dissension among the Whigs. It was his first mistake as President.

The Cabinet's loyalties lay elsewhere than with Tyler, as later events proved. He himself said he was "surrounded by Clay-men, Webster-men, anti-Masons, original Harrisonians, old Whigs and new Whigs— each jealous of the other, and all struggling for the offices." Before the year was out, these conflicting loyalties would create a White House crisis.

During that first Cabinet meeting, Tyler set the tone of his administration. Webster, the Secretary of State, told the President that Harrison had submitted all policy decisions to a Cabinet vote. This conformed to Jefferson's conception of the Cabinet, "in which the President counts himself but one."

"I beg your pardon, gentlemen," Tyler replied, rising, "I am the President, and I shall be held responsible for my administration. I shall be pleased to avail myself of your counsel and advice. But I can never consent to being dictated to as to what I shall or shall not do." He looked around at the six men gathered in the room and added, "When you think otherwise, your resignations will be accepted."

Tyler did not have to wait long to have his leadership tested. On May 31st Congress convened in a special session which had been called by Harrison before he died. One of the first resolutions in the House was to address Tyler as "Vice-President, now exercising the duties of President." It was overridden. The next day a similar resolution was defeated in the Senate by a vote of 38 to 8. This was a nonpartisan victory for Tyler because the Whig majority at the time was only four.

"So far things go on smoothly," the President wrote to a friend, "and but for the currency question, the course would be tranquil. There lies the rub."

It was a substantial rub. The "currency question" dated back to 1791 when the first Bank of the United States had been chartered by Congress for 20 years. The Bank was privately owned and operated, and it was authorized to hold government funds, issue currency and establish branches in the various states. The South opposed the Bank vigorously. Jefferson correctly pointed out that the Constitution made no provision for such a bank. Hamilton argued that justification for the Bank could be found in the Constitution's "implied powers." Washington accepted Hamilton's loose construction of the Constitution and signed the Bank bill into law. In 1816 the second Bank of the United States was chartered for another 20 years (Congress had rejected a charter renewal in 1811). But the second Bank's operations were tarnished by scandal and speculation, and in 1832 Andrew Jackson vetoed a bill to renew its charter. Since then the bank issue had been a political football.

Tyler consistently had opposed a national bank on constitutional grounds (although he had been discreetly silent on the issue during the election). Now he wished to defer broaching the issue. "I have no

intention to submit anything to Congress on this subject to be acted on," he told Clay, "but shall leave
it to its own action."

This was consistent with Tyler's belief that the President's function was to inform Congress, not to lead it.
He soon learned how mistaken he was. An absence
of leadership in politics creates a vacuum which
somebody is always willing to fill. In this case, Senator
Henry Clay, his eyes glued to the 1844 Whig presidential nomination, was ready to lead Congress *and*
Tyler, whom he regarded as a "flash in the pan."

Clay, who long had favored a national bank, was
certain he now could push his own program through
Congress and over Tyler. Remarked one observer of
Clay: "He is more imperious and arrogant with his
friends than I have ever known him, and that, you
know, is saying a great deal."

Quickly, Clay moved into the power vacuum and
took charge of the Whig majority. On July 28th he
steered the District Bank bill through the Senate, 26
to 23. A few days later the House approved the
measure 131 to 100.

Everyone wondered whether or not Tyler would
veto the bill. "Nothing is thought of, dreamed upon,
or sworn about now but the fate of the bank bill,"
reported the New York *Herald*.

Webster and the rest of the Cabinet "all earnestly
recommended the President to sign the bill." A Whig
Congressman told Tyler, "If you can reconcile this bill
to yourself, all is sunshine and calm: your administration will be met by the warm, hearty, zealous support

of the whole Whig party, and when you retire from the great theatre of National politics, it will be with the thanks and plaudits, and approbation of your countrymen."

But Tyler never had been concerned with popularity. "Whether I sink or swim on the tide of popular favor," he once said, "is a matter to me of inferior consideration." By now he saw the bank issue as a test of will between himself and Clay, the Executive and Congress. "My back is to the wall," he told a friend, adding, "I shall, if practicable, beat back the assailants."

On August 16th, Tyler vetoed the District Bank bill on constitutional grounds. "It will suffice to say that my own opinion has been uniformly proclaimed to be against the exercise of any such power by this government," he said. Whig demonstrators hanged him in effigy, and Clay suggested that the President resign, but the veto was sustained in the Senate.

Clay was undaunted. The Whigs quickly produced another bank measure, the Fiscal Corporation bill. This bill was drafted by the Cabinet (four of whom were Clay men), ostensibly to remove the President's constitutional objections to a bank measure. But the bill, as passed in the House, 125 to 94, and in the Senate, 27 to 22, retained those features which Tyler considered unconstitutional. No matter, thought Clay.

"Tyler dare not resist," the Great Compromiser told a friend of the President, "I will drive him before me!"

"You are mistaken, Mr. Clay," the friend replied. "Mr. Tyler wants to approve the Bill, but he thinks his oath is in the way, and I, who know him very well, will tell you that when he thinks he is right, he is as obstinate as a bull, and no power on earth can move him."

The friend proved to be right. On September 9th, Tyler vetoed the Fiscal Corporation bill on the same constitutional grounds he had cited for the previous bill, adding to his veto message a defense of the executive use of the veto power. Two days later, at Clay's instigation, the Secretaries of Treasury, War, Navy, the Postmaster General and the Attorney General marched, one by one, into the President's office and laid their resignations on his desk. Tyler's son, John, standing by with a pocket watch, recorded the exact time of each resignation.

The sixth Cabinet member, Webster, also made an appearance. "Where am I to go, Mr. President?" the Secretary of State asked in his deep, booming voice.

"You must decide that for yourself, Mr. Webster," Tyler replied.

"If you leave it to me, Mr. President," said Webster, "I will stay where I am."

The President rose from his chair and extended his hand. "Give me your hand on that," he said, "and now I will say to you that Henry Clay is a doomed man."

He didn't know how right he was.

The Cabinet resignations of September 11th were timed to cripple the executive branch of the government and bring Tyler himself to the brink of resignation. Congress was scheduled to adjourn for three months on Monday, September 13th. That left the

President only one day, Sunday, to select a new Cabinet, for appointees always had been confirmed by the Senate before it adjourned. If Tyler failed to meet the deadline, he would be without five department heads for three months. Unable to run the government under such circumstances, he might be constrained to resign.

So Clay reasoned. But Tyler had been considering replacing the Cabinet anyway, and he quickly appointed his own men to the vacated posts. The Senate confirmed the appointments the next day. (As it turned out, the President had little better luck with his own appointees. In less than four years, twenty men held the six Cabinet posts, a record which never has been equaled.)

Tyler's swift action in the Cabinet crisis assured the continued functioning of the executive branch of the government. The Whigs, frustrated again, then issued an extraordinary public statement officially repudiating Tyler and all his actions. This unique act in the history of American politics left Tyler, in Clay's words, a "President without a party" and killed any chance he had of winning the 1844 presidential nomination on his own.

The Whig extremists had one more insult left. In January, 1843, they introduced in the House a resolution to appoint a committee to draw up an impeachment of the President. Nine specific charges of "high crimes and misdemeanors" were singled out for investigation. Actually, they were indictments of Tyler's interpretation of the functions of the executive and legislative branches of government, with which the congressional Whigs disagreed. The resolution was voted down, 127–84, and impeachment of a President was forestalled for a quarter of a century.

Until then the Administration had functioned, in Tyler's words, "amid earthquake and tornado," and it had failed to enact any significant legislation. "The difficulty in the way of administering the government without a party is undoubtedly great," the President admitted. He had preserved the independence and prerogatives of the Executive, but in the process he had forfeited the cooperation of Congress, his own political future and even his good name. Now he devoted himself to one last task which, if successful, might salvage the historical reputation of his administration. That task was the annexation of Texas to the United States.

Texas had declared its independence from Mexico in 1836. The following year the new republic's petition for annexation to the United States was refused. Since then, annexation had been stalemated by the slavery issue. Northerners feared that several slave states might be carved out of the huge Texas territory and upset the free and slave state balance of power which had been preserved by the Missouri Compromise in 1820.

That bill admitted to the Union Maine and Missouri, a free and a slave state, and excluded slavery in the Louisiana Territory north of the 36° 30′ parallel. The Compromise was more of a southern concession than a compromise, for it established the right of Congress to exclude slavery from the territories and left the bulk of the Louisiana Territory free. It was a fatal weakening of the South's political position on slavery. Tyler was one of the few Southerners to realize this in 1820. He consistently voted against the bill in Congress. "For myself, I cannot and will not yield one inch of the ground," he said. Unfortunately, he offered no reasonable alternatives.

Tyler defended the existence of the "peculiar institution" of slavery, but he did not seek its perpetuation, as did men like Calhoun. Tyler's own theory was that if slavery were allowed to spread to the territories it would diminish in strength and gradually disappear, like a drop of ink in a pond. But that was not why he was for the annexation of Texas. He wanted the glory of moving the country's frontier farther west: "If the annexation of Texas shall crown off my public life," he said, "I shall neither retire ignominiously nor be soon forgotten."

Tyler already had settled the smoldering Main-New Brunswick border dispute by the Webster-Ashburton Treaty in 1842. This treaty, by removing the threat of war with Britain, cleared the way for settlement of the Texas question. Webster himself, however, could not support Texas annexation; and he resigned as Secretary of State in May, 1843. Tyler chose as the New Englander's replacement Abel P. Upshur, a brilliant Southerner who was dedicated to annexation.

Mexico, of course, still regarded Texas as Mexican territory. In August, 1843, Mexican President Santa Anna warned Tyler that he would consider annexation of Texas "equivalent to a declaration of war

against the Mexican Republic." Tyler negotiated with
the Texans anyway.

In January, 1844, Upshur informed the Texans that
"a clear constitutional majority of two-thirds" of the
Senate favored annexation. If he was right, it would
have been a remarkable victory for Tyler, for the Whigs
still controlled the Senate. But the test was delayed
when, in February, Upshur was killed by a cannon explosion on the naval frigate *Princeton*. The President
himself only narrowly escaped death. He was on his
way to witness the firing of the cannon when he stopped
momentarily to catch the refrain of a song below decks.
Seconds later the cannon exploded, killing eight specta-
tors.

Among the victims of the accident was Senator
David Gardiner, whose daughter, Julia, the President
had been courting. Tyler's first wife, Letitia, had died
in 1842 after 29 years of marriage.

Julia Gardiner was beautiful, vivacious and only
twenty-four, 30 years younger than the graying
President. She brought gaiety, wit and charm
wherever she went—and she went to the White House
as often as the President could arrange a chaperoned
visit. Tyler played cards with her, squired her home
from church and even "flew down the stairs" of the
White House "after her around chairs and tables until
at last he caught her." He called Julia his "fairy girl"
and spoke of his "dreamy anticipation" of her letters
to him. In April, 1844, he formally asked Mrs.
Gardiner for Julia's hand in marriage. "My position
in Society will, I trust, serve as a guarantee for the appearance which I give," he wrote. It did. On June 26,

1844, four months after the *Princeton* tragedy, Julia Gardiner and John Tyler were married in New York. This first marriage of a President in office lasted until Tyler's death in 1862 and produced seven children.

In the Cabinet, Upshur was succeeded by Calhoun. Predictably, the fiery South Carolinian stirred the smoldering ashes of the slavery issue, convincing many Northerners that the annexation of Texas was a pro-slavery plot. When the Texas treaty came before the Senate on April 22, 1844, the Administration's hopes for passage were dim. A few days later, both Clay and Van Buren, the expected presidential nominees of their parties, came out against annexation. Clay called the move "dangerous to the integrity of the Union, in-expedient in the present financial condition of the country, and not called for by any general expression of public opinion." Strictly speaking, Clay was cor-rect, but Americans can be thankful that Tyler was adamant.

The Whig convention nominated Clay for the presi-dency by acclamation on May 1st. In typical Whig fashion, the Texas issue was not even mentioned in the party platform. Tyler now moved to apply political pressure on the Democrats, many of whom, as South-erners, favored annexation. He instructed his followers to nominate him for the presidency under the banner of a third party, hoping to use as a lever the small bloc of votes he could be expected to draw: if the Demo-crats would endorse annexation, Tyler would withdraw from the race and throw his support to the Democratic nominee.

Tyler had toyed with the idea of a third party since

1841. At first he thought such an organization might return him to the White House in 1844. But he soon realized that he could not create a party strong enough to do that. By 1844 Tyler "entertained no hope of an election himself"; he ran for the "sole purpose of controlling events"—that is, bargaining with the Democrats.

The Democratic Convention met in Baltimore on May 27th to nominate a candidate. Van Buren, whose opposition to annexation had alienated the party patriarch, Andrew Jackson, led on the first ballot, but he fell 31 votes short of the two-thirds majority necessary for nomination. Then the Convention deadlocked. Seven ballots were taken, but no candidate was able to command a two-thirds majority. The delegates returned to their whiskey and cigars to hammer out a compromise. Meanwhile, Tyler's third party, convening nearby, quickly nominated the President to shouts of "Tyler and Texas!"

On the ninth ballot the Democrats chose the first dark-horse candidate in convention history, James K. Polk—a slaveowner and annexationist. The party platform urged "the reannexation of Texas at the earliest practicable period." Tyler had succeeded.

However, on June 8th, the Senate voted 35–16 against ratification of the annexation treaty. The two-thirds majority in favor of annexation, which Upshur had lined up in January, had become, in the few months of Calhoun's stewardship, a two-thirds majority *against* the treaty!

Tyler moved to circumvent the Senate. He introduced a measure to annex Texas by a joint resolution of Congress, which required only a majority of one vote in each house to pass. It was the second instance in which Tyler, the strict constructionist, had broadened his interpretation of the Constitution.

Clay now tried to straddle the issue of annexation. On July 27th he stated that "far from having any personal objection to the annexation of Texas, I should be glad to see it . . . upon just and fair terms." He was too late—and, as events proved, he was moving in the wrong direction. On August 20th Tyler officially withdrew from the race and threw his support to Polk. Ten days later, a splinter group of antislavery northern Whigs calling themselves the Liberty Party nominated for the presidency James G. Birney, a New York abolitionist and anti-annexationist. As it turned out, Birney, not Tyler, decided the election.

During the heat of the campaign the Whigs asked derisively, "Who is James K. Polk?" In November, the electorate answered: the 11th President of the United States. Polk edged Clay by 38,175 popular votes, 65 electoral votes. He carried New York's 36 electoral votes—the difference between victory and defeat—by only 5,080 votes. Birney polled 15,812 votes in New York. Half of these—enough for victory—might have gone to Clay if he had maintained his anti-annexation stand of April!

The defeat finished Clay as a serious contender for the presidency.

Congress had adjourned before acting on the joint resolution for annexation, so Tyler resubmitted the measure when the legislature reconvened in December. He considered the election results a mandate for annexation. "It is the will of the people and the states," he said, "that Texas shall be annexed to the Union promptly and immediately."

For the next three months the President, his family and friends lobbied incessantly to line up the necessary votes in Congress for annexation. Time was running out, for British diplomats in Mexico City were busy arranging an entente between Mexico and Texas which would make Texas an independent "buffer" state and block America's westward expansion.

On February 27th the Senate narrowly passed the measure, 27–25. A single vote switch would have defeated it. Twenty-four hours later, the House concurred, 132–76. The resolution granted Texas immediate statehood and extended the Missouri Compromise line of 36° 30′ into the new state. On March 1, 1845, only three days before his term of office expired, Tyler signed the measure into law.

A few weeks later the British persuaded Mexico to recognize Texan independence on the condition that Texas relinquish annexation to the United States. If Congress had not acted when it did, Texas might have accepted the Mexican terms (and British financial assistance). An independent Texas might have shut off the United States from the entire Southwest and California (which were then part of the Mexican Empire). The country would look very different today. That it doesn't can be attributed to Tyler's persistence, a New York abolitionist's candidacy and one Senate vote. Such are the factors that direct a nation's destiny.

So ended the term of the first Vice-President to

succeed to the presidency. John Tyler retired to his Virginia plantation, Sherwood Forest, only two miles away from Greenway, where he had grown up. At Sherwood Forest he played the role of elder statesman, raised a family, rode through the fields overseeing his crops, shot deer and "fiddled" for the plantation children or anyone who would listen. In 1861 he urged Virginia's secession from the Union. The next year he died in Richmond, where he had gone to take a seat in the Confederate House of Representatives.

Tyler's impact on the presidency is seldom recognized. Sectional loyalties prevented him from exercising the full moral force of the presidency. But he preserved the power of the Executive at a time when the majority of Congress insisted that the Executive was "dependent upon and responsible to" the Legislative. "Each branch of the government is independent of every other," Tyler argued, "and heaven forbid that the day should ever come when either can dictate to the other."

The vice-presidency continued to be held in disdain, but Tyler left an important legacy to those who would follow him. "Future Vice-Presidents who may succeed to the presidency," he said, "may feel some slight encouragement to pursue an independent course."

*It is not out of hostility to you or your Adminis-
tration but . . . for the best interest of the country.*

—MILLARD FILLMORE to
President Taylor explaining
his support of the Compromise of 1850

2 Millard Fillmore: 1850

It wasn't long before the flag was again at half-mast
over the White House. Tyler's successor, Polk, true to
an 1844 promise, declined to run for a second term as
President. "I am heartily rejoiced that my term is so
near its close," he wrote in his diary. "I will soon cease
to be a servant and become a sovereign."

And so, in 1848, began the long, hard quest for the
presidency by a number of sovereigns eager to become
servants.

1848 was the year of the generals in presidential
politics. Recalling their success with "Old Tippecanoe," the Whigs nominated for President "Old
Rough n' Ready" General Zachary Taylor, whose vic-
tories in the recently concluded Mexican War had made
him a popular hero. The Democrats countered with
General Lewis Cass, who had served with Harrison in
the Indian campaigns. Cass's running mate was General William O. Butler, who had fought under Jackson

at New Orleans and under Taylor at Monterrey. Into this parade of old soldiers stepped Taylor's running mate, Millard Fillmore, a former commander of the Buffalo Home Guard. Of the four, he was destined to play the largest role in the nation's affairs.

Fillmore was a politician from upstate New York who believed in expressing his indifference to an office before running for it. He was a self-educated, self-made man. Born in 1800 in a rude log cabin, he spent his boyhood on the family farm, reaping and clearing land for crops in what were then the virgin forests of central New York. Somehow he learned to read, and he quickly exhausted the family library, a Bible, a hymn book and an almanac. As a youth he was apprenticed to a clothmaker—"It made me feel for the weak and unprotected," he later wrote—and he read law with a local judge. He also taught school, although he had attended it only infrequently.

When Fillmore was twenty-three he was admitted to the bar in Buffalo, which was then a booming frontier town awaiting the opening of the Erie Canal. Three years later he married his longtime sweetheart, a schoolteacher who had helped him with his intermittent studies. It was a happy marriage. "For twenty-seven years, my entire married life," Fillmore later said, "I was always greeted with a happy smile."

Together, the Fillmores began to collect books and acquaintances, and as the eager young lawyer learned to conform to the opinions and habits of "civilized" society, he gradually drifted into politics. In 1828, under the banner of the Anti-Masons, he was elected

to the state legislature in Albany. There he became a
protege of the newspaper editor and political boss,
Thurlow Weed. Weed, and the Buffalo electorate, sub-
sequently sent him to Congress for four terms.

Success did not spoil him. He was one of those
genial, plodding, predictable men who fill the oak-
paneled chambers of legislative bodies across the nation. Ambition led him on, but it did not goad him.
He was more interested in comfort and dignity than in
glory.

For comfort and dignity there was nothing like the
vice-presidency of the United States, so in 1842 Fillmore resigned his seat in the House to concentrate on
becoming Clay's running mate in 1844. In a parting
salvo at President Tyler, whom he had opposed assidu-

ously, he described the former Vice-President's succession to the presidency as "an awful warning to select no man, even for a contingent station of such vast power and responsibility, whose talents and integrity are not equal to it."

The Whigs appeared to take Fillmore at his word; they passed him up for the 1844 vice-presidential nomination. As a consolation Fillmore ran for Governor of New York. It didn't matter. Clay lost New York and the election, and Fillmore ran almost 5,000 votes behind Clay. "The Abolitionists and foreign Catholics have defeated us," Fillmore told Weed. "May God save the country," he added dolefully, "for it is evident the people will not."

Four years later General Taylor stepped forward to do the job. "I have consented to the use of my name as a candidate for the presidency," he stated publicly six weeks before the Whig Convention, adding, "I have frankly avowed my own distrust of my fitness for that high station. . . ." Some Whigs were inclined to agree on that point. One of them said that Old Zack's qualifications consisted of "sleeping forty years in the woods and cultivating moss on the calves of his legs." But he was the candidate who most appealed to most of the people. "We can elect nobody but General Taylor," said a young Illinois Whig, Abraham Lincoln, and in June the convention made the sixty-four-year-old war hero and cotton planter its choice on the fourth ballot.

Once again Fillmore sought the vice-presidential nomination. By this time his relations with Weed had cooled as a result of Weed's clear preference for a rival protege, the sharp, aggressive William H. Seward. Weed, in fact, wanted Seward for the second spot on the ticket, but the former Governor wasn't interested. So Weed offered the nomination to Daniel Webster. "No thank you," said the great orator, rejecting what proved to be his last chance to gain the presidency he coveted so much, "I don't propose to be buried until I am really dead and in my coffin."

The Taylor Whigs wanted to balance the ticket with Abbott Lawrence, a wealthy Massachusetts textile manufacturer. But the Clay Whigs refused to tolerate "cotton at both ends of the ticket," so to placate Clay's followers, the delegates voted for Fillmore over Lawrence, 115 to 109, on the first ballot, then gave the New Yorker a winning majority on the second one. Had Lawrence manufactured toothpicks instead of textiles, he probably would have become the 13th President of the United States. Such are the small ironies of history.

Official notice of his nomination was mailed to Taylor in Baton Rouge. But since the General had notified the local postmaster that he no longer would accept "postage due" letters, the news was forwarded to the dead-letter office. Finally, after several weeks of embarrassing silence, Taylor surmised what had happened, retrieved the letter and dispatched a formal acceptance of the nomination. The Whigs praised their candidate's frugality; the Democrats snickered at "economical, comical Old Zack."

Slavery and its extension were the overriding issues

of the campaign. California and New Mexico, which had been acquired from Mexico, were eager to join the Union. But their admittance hinged on whether or not slavery would be extended to their territories. In 1846, David Wilmot, a Pennsylvania Democrat, had introduced in the House a measure which would exclude slavery from any territory obtained from Mexico. The Wilmot Proviso, as it was called, was tacked onto a bill providing funds for possible negotiations with Mexico. It passed in the House but not in the Senate, where the South had enough power to vote it down. Since then the Proviso had been like a cocked pistol aimed at the South, with the North seeking enough Senate votes to pull the trigger.

General Cass opposed the Wilmot Proviso. He was for "squatter sovereignty"—local determination of the status of slavery—and against federal "interference" with slavery in the states. Taylor, a slave owner himself, was for slavery but not for its expansion. As a candidate, he wisely tiptoed around the issue. "Let this vexed question remain where the Constitution placed it," he said enigmatically. He sought to walk the middle of the road to the Promised Land. "If I am elected," he said, in what is considered his most effective campaign statement, "I shall do all that an honest zeal may effect to cement the bonds of our Union and establish the happiness of my countrymen upon an enduring basis." And he assured the voters that he was not "a party candidate" in the sense "which would prevent my being the President of the whole people."

General Taylor has come down through the his-

tories as a rough-edged, blundering campaigner whom
the Whigs had to muzzle for his own good. That is not
true. Actually Taylor was a hundred years ahead of
his time. He knew that the Whigs were a minority
party, and he tried to appeal to the voter beyond party
lines. His campaign—indeed, his personality and his
conception of the presidency—resembled remarkably
General Eisenhower's.

Taylor remained in Louisiana, playing it cool, and
most of the campaigning fell to Fillmore. Twelve years
previously Fillmore had gone on record as being in
favor of Congress abolishing the interstate slave trade.
Now, as southern Democrats branded him an "abolitionist," he was hard pressed to match Taylor's delicate
neutrality. But he quickly proved that art is long,
memory short. He "regarded slavery as an evil," he
told the southern doubters, "but one with which the
National Government has nothing to do." The resolution of the question of slavery, he added, lay with
"the several states where the institution was tolerated.
If they regarded it as a blessing, they had a constitutional right to enjoy it; and if they regarded it as an
evil, they had the power and knew best how to apply
the remedy."

Such fancy footwork was hard to beat—as Generals
Cass and Butler discovered on election day. The decisive factor in the election, however, proved to be a
deep split in the ranks of the Democratic Party. Antislavery Democrats in New York, disgusted by Cass's
outspoken opposition to the Wilmot Proviso, bolted the
party and formed their own Free Soil Party. They

were joined by the antislavery Whigs who had formed the Liberty Party in 1844. Martin Van Buren, the old Van of Kinderhook, was their candidate. Van Buren didn't carry a single state, but he did split the Democratic vote in New York enough for Taylor to carry the state. Once again, New York's 36 electoral votes were the margin of victory. The final electoral count was Taylor 163, Cass 127.

With Taylor's victory came the Whig scramble for patronage. The power of appointment is one of the most potent weapons in the presidential arsenal, as Jackson proved with his "spoils system." But Taylor (like Eisenhower a century later) deplored this aspect of politics. "I wish Mr. Fillmore would take all of the business into his own hands," Taylor told a friend.

Fillmore was willing, even eager, to do this, but Weed and Seward had other plans. New York's Senator John A. Dix was about to retire, and Weed pushed Seward's candidacy for the vacant Senate seat. This would give Seward—and Weed—a power base in Washington, for a Senator traditionally has a voice in the patronage of his state.

Seward's principal contender for the seat was John A. Collier, an ally of Fillmore's and a strong anti-Weed man. At that time, Senators were elected by the state legislatures. Weed audaciously approached Fillmore to use his influence in Albany to elect Seward. He pledged in return to share the state patronage with the Vice-President. Fillmore, despite Weed's clear record of treachery, naively agreed to share a power he already had within his grasp. With the Vice-President's support, Seward beat Collier and went on to Washington, where he swiftly undermined Fillmore's influence within the Administration.

Almost immediately after Seward's election, the Vice-President was wishing "that he could exchange places with the Senator-elect." He had discovered that a Senator had more power than the Vice-President—except in one respect. John Adams had expressed it neatly when he said, "I am Vice-President. In this I am nothing, but I may be everything."

Taylor was now everything—and finding it troublesome. The "vexed question" of slavery refused to "remain where the Constitution had placed it"—wherever that was. California, brought to the brink of anarchy by the 1849 Gold Rush, was clamoring for some kind of stable government. But slave or free? Congress still had not resolved the question. Meanwhile, Texas, with the support of the southern slave states, was threatening to impose its claims on the New Mexico territory with troops. Southerners talked openly of secession and civil war unless they got concessions on these issues.

When Congress convened in December of 1849, Taylor revealed his plans in two messages to the assembled legislators. He recommended immediate statehood for California and New Mexico. This would avoid the agitation over slavery which would be aroused by first organizing them as territories. As for the Union, "whatever dangers may threaten it," he said, "I shall stand by it and maintain its integrity to the full extent of the obligations imposed and the powers conferred upon me by the Constitution."

Theoretically, under Taylor's plan, the two new states would make their own decisions on slavery. But California, as Taylor well knew, recently had adopted a constitution which prohibited slavery, and New Mexico was unsuitable for growing cotton, the *raison d'etre* of slavery. So in practice, California and New Mexico would come into the Union as free states, upsetting the traditional balance of free and slave states.

Southerners were outraged. They denounced Taylor as a traitor to his class and to his region. But the General never had been "a southern candidate." During the campaign he shrewdly had maintained an enigmatic neutrality on the slavery issue, allowing Southerners and Northerners alike to read into his position what they wished. Now Southerners discovered that they had not read the fine print: Taylor's unwavering devotion to the Union.

Into the battle which was shaping up, stepped a figure out of the past, the Great Compromiser, Henry Clay. The gaunt Kentuckian, now seventy-three years old and in the waning years of his life, only recently had returned to the Senate. On Tuesday, January 29, 1850, he took the Senate floor to propose his last great compromise.

"I hold in my hand," Clay announced, "a series of resolutions which I desire to submit to the consideration of this body. . . ." He offered eight resolutions. They key proposals provided for California's admission to the Union as a free state, the organization of New Mexico and Deseret (Utah) as territories in which slavery would not be restricted, the adjustment of the Texas-New Mexico boundary, the abolition of the slave trade in the District of Columbia and the "more effectual provision" for "restitution and delivery" of fugitive slaves.

Holding aloft a fragment of George Washington's coffin, Clay invoked the spirit of the first President to preserve the Union. The Senate agreed to open debate on Clay's measures on the following Tuesday.

Thus was the stage set for the greatest debate in the history of Congress. All of Clay's resolutions except the one on California ran counter to the President's plan either in letter or in spirit. Especially irreconcilable were Clay's proposal to organize New Mexico and Utah into *territories* and Taylor's plan to admit them as *states,* skipping the provisional territorial stage. The battle lines were drawn; Congress would have to choose between the two programs.

The 31st Congress was perhaps the most illustrious in the nation's history. In addition to the famed triumvirate of Clay, Calhoun and Webster, the Senate included the fiery Thomas Hart Benton, his tormentor, the peppery Mississippian, Henry S. Foote, Jefferson Davis, Sam Houston, Stephen A. Douglas, General Cass (again a Michigan Senator), and, of course, the swiftly rising Seward. Democrats outnumbered Whigs in the House by 112 to 109; but the balance of power was held by 13 Free-Soilers. The House was so divided that it took three weeks and *63* ballots to elect a

Speaker. In the Senate the Democrats had a majority of ten.

Tuesday came, a "brilliant and sparkling winter's morning." Visitors flocked to the Senate chamber to hear the opening of the Great Debate. They packed the galleries and overflowed onto the floor of the chamber. Clay slowly walked up Capitol Hill, leaning on the arm of a friend, occasionally pausing to cough or catch his breath. As he pushed his way into the crowded chamber, the buzzing of voices momentarily subsided, then quickened. Fillmore, presiding over the Senate, directed the transaction of the Senate's routine business. Then he recognized the Senator from Kentucky. A hush fell over the chamber as the slender, white-haired Clay took the floor to speak.

"Never, on any former occasion," Clay began, "have I risen under feelings of such deep solicitude. . . ." He defended his eight resolutions, warning that the alternative would be a "disastrous leap . . . into the yawning abyss below." Sam Houston supported him. His southern heart, Houston assured Congress, was large enough "to embrace the whole Union, if not the whole world." Just like a Texan. Jefferson Davis opposed any concessions to the North. Calhoun, dying from tuberculosis, argued against the President's plan and Clay's Compromise and called for secession if "you reduce the question to submission or resistance." Webster replied in his memorable 7th of March speech: "I wish to speak today not as a Massachusetts man, nor as a northern man, but as an American." He asked for concessions on both sides. Seward attacked the idea of compromise, proclaiming, "There is a higher law than the Constitution."

Fillmore, as President of the Senate, could not take part in the debate. He listened to the arguments of both sides and tried to make up his own mind. "It may come to my casting vote," he told a friend, "as to that —*Quaere?* I shall wait till I see what shape it assumes before I determine to say yea or nay."

For five months the debate raged. Personal insults, and even punches, were exchanged by the debaters. At one point, Fillmore was forced to lecture the Senate on its conduct. "Many little irregularities," he said, "may be tolerated in a small body that would cause much disorder in a large one." It was a masterpiece of understatement.

By July, the situation looked like a dangerous stalemate. The President could not muster enough congressional support for his plan; but if Clay squeezed the Compromise through Congress, Taylor could veto the bill and Clay would be unable to secure enough Senate votes to override the veto. Meanwhile, nine slave states had met in convention in Nashville, Tennessee, to discuss secession, and Texas was threatening to send troops to New Mexico to "arrest" the United States officers there. "The cause of Texas will be the cause of the entire South," declared one Congressman, adding, "When the 'Rubicon' is passed, the days of this Republic will be numbered."

The country seemed headed toward civil war. Then fate intervened. At an Independence Day ceremony, the President exposed himself to the sun's oppressive heat for two hours, then gulped some cold cherries and milk. He became ill with what was diagnosed as cholera, which was prevalent in the country at that time.

Taylor had overcome a similar attack the previous year, and one of his doctors expressed himself "not frightened by the symptoms." The patient felt differently. "In two days," Taylor muttered on July 7th, "I shall be a dead man." His timing was perfect. On Tuesday, July 9th, with the words, "I regret nothing, but am sorry that I am about to leave my friends," he died. It was 10:35 P.M.

The mantle of the presidency passed on to Fillmore. A messenger from the Cabinet immediately brought word of Taylor's death to Fillmore at his hotel room. Thanks to the precedent Tyler had set, the official message was addressed to Millard Fillmore, "President of the United States."

The new President did not sleep that night. "I was oppressed by a sense of the great responsibilities that rested upon me," he later wrote, "and sincerely distrusted my ability."

Fillmore had every right to doubt himself. He had succeeded to the world's most demanding executive job in the eleventh hour of a crisis—with not a minute of executive experience. All his training had been in legislative work. He was an experienced politician, and this would help in the White House. But even his grasp of politics didn't match his years of experience in it, as indicated by his unwise support of Seward's Senate candidacy. Were Fillmore's political talents broad enough to lead the nation through this sectional crisis? Americans of moderate persuasion prayed that they were.

There was hope. Compromise ran deeper than conviction in the new President. As Vice-President, Fillmore had begun to lean strongly toward Clay's bill. "I might be called upon to give a casting vote in the Senate on the Compromise Bill," he told Taylor shortly before the President's death, "and if I should feel it my duty to vote for it, as I might, I wish you to understand that it is not out of hostility to you or your Administration but . . . for the best interests of the country."

But now he himself was President, and his responsibility was greater. Through the hot summer night he wrestled with the problem. In the end he settled for compromise. He knew he was jeopardizing his political future. But, he said, "to me this is nothing. The man who can look upon a crisis without being willing to offer himself upon the altar of his country is not fit for public trust." And so Fillmore walked calmly to the altar.

The next day Millard Fillmore took the oath as 13th President of the United States. Six feet tall, stocky and straight-backed, he cut an impressive figure. His full face, shock of white hair and friendly blue eyes gave him the appearance of a fatherly statesman. He looked like a man who would be comfortable with a good cigar, a glass of port and a few attentive friends.

Taylor's Cabinet promptly resigned in a body. Fillmore wisely accepted the resignations. "I knew," he said later, "that their policy was not such as I could approve." To the most influential Cabinet post, Secretary of State, he appointed Daniel Webster. It was the second time Webster would serve a man who had gained the coveted presidency via the office which he himself had dismissed as a dead end. What thoughts crossed Webster's mind on this occasion can only be guessed; outwardly, he rejoiced over the turn of events in the nation's crisis. "I believe Mr. Fillmore favors the Compromise," he said, "and there is no doubt that recent events"—Taylor's death—"have increased the probability of the passage of that measure."

That was Clay's feeling, too, so he forced the Compromise to a Senate vote on July 31st. He lost. One section of the bill after another was struck down: 33 to 22 against the New Mexico territorial arrangement, 29 to 28 against the Texas-New Mexico boundary, 34 to 25 against statehood for California. Only the section on Utah passed.

The situation was blacker than ever. Clay, physically exhausted, went to Rhode Island to rest. His leadership was assumed by Stephen A. Douglas, who now proposed to submit the compromise measures one by one, in separate bills. On August 6th, President Fillmore delivered to Congress a message which outlined the executive position on the issues. It was one of the state papers which, says historian Richard B. Morris, "shaped the course of history."

In his message Fillmore dispassionately reviewed the explosive Texas-New Mexico boundary issue. New Mexico is under the jurisdiction of the United States, he explained, and any aggressive action by Texas "militia" or "civil posse" would be met promptly by federal armed force. "Neither the Constitution nor the laws nor my duty nor my oath of office leave me any alternative or any choice in my mode of action," he said. He urged Congress to settle the Texas boundary dispute during the current session "in any other mode which the wisdom of Congress may devise"— that is, along the lines of Clay's Compromise. "The settlement of other questions connected with the same subject within the same period," he added, "is greatly to be desired."

Fillmore's message—plus his astute use of the patronage power—was decisive in persuading Congress to reconsider the Compromise. He had done what Taylor had failed to do and what historian Richard E. Neustadt calls "the essence of a President's persuasive task with congressmen and everybody else"—namely, "to induce them to believe that what he wants of them is what their own appraisal of their own responsibilities requires them to do in their interest, not in his." It is no mean accomplishment, as many Presidents have discovered.

One week after Fillmore's message the Senate voted 34 to 18 to admit California to the Union as a free state. The House concurred 150 to 56. Within a month, Congress enacted four more separate compromise bills. New Mexico was organized as a territory, without restriction on slavery, and Texas was paid $10 million to relinquish its claims on New Mexico. Utah was made a territory under similar terms. The slave trade was abolished in the District of Columbia. And a fugitive slave act was passed. Fillmore signed each bill into law.

The Union had been preserved—temporarily—but Fillmore's worries continued. That usually is the fate of the President. On the domestic front, Northerners agitated against the Fugitive Slave Law. It was an inhuman law, as slavery was an inhuman practice, but Fillmore felt that he was constitutionally obliged to uphold it. "I mean at all hazards to do my part towards executing this law," he said. "I admit no right of *nullification* North or South."

Foreign affairs were humming, too, in Hungary and Cuba. Curiously enough, events there were previews of almost identical situations which would arise to haunt Americans 100-odd years later. Even more amazing is the fact that the results of these actions, separated by a century in time, were so similar.

Hungarian nationalists, under a Magyar nobleman, Louis Kossuth, had revolted against Austrian domination in 1848. Taylor had sent a secret agent to the revolutionary regime to assure it of United States recognition—if the revolt succeeded. It didn't. Czar Nicholas I sent a Russian army to help the Austrians subdue the Hungarian nationalists, a job which Soviet tanks would do alone 107 years later!

Somehow, the Austrian government discovered the purpose of the American agent's mission. Chevalier J. G. Hulsemann, Austrian charge d'affaires in Washington, protested to Taylor and then to Secretary of

State Webster in 1850 that the United States was "impatient for the downfall of the Austrian monarchy."

Webster, with Fillmore's approval, replied that the United States had a right to take an interest in European revolutions, which "appeared to have their origin in those great ideas of responsible and popular governments on which the American constitutions themselves are founded." Furthermore, Webster boasted, American power now extended over a region "in comparison with which the possessions of the House of Hapsburg are but as a patch on the earth's surface." So much for the Austrian Empire!

Meanwhile, Fillmore had his hands full with American filibusters. These were not the parliamentary stalling tactics made famous by the United States Senate but adventures in which guerrilla expeditions purposely fomented revolutions in Central and South America. The word filibuster is adapted from the Spanish *filibustero,* which means "freebooter." And indeed, though some nineteenth-century filibusterers genuinely were concerned with freedom, most of them sought personal power and plunder. One of these was General Narciso López, a Venezuelan adventurer who claimed that the Cuban people were ready to revolt against their Spanish oppressors.

Many Americans—especially Southerners—found it profitable to agree with López. American expansionists had coveted Cuba for many years, and Southerners saw the island as a fertile ground for cotton and slavery. In 1848 Polk had offered Spain $100 million for Cuba. Now southern annexationists backed expeditions that would provoke a Cuban "revolution" which, as in the case of Texas, would end in American statehood.

Twice during Taylor's administration López, with southern backing, had organized Cuban filibusters. Both had ended in fiasco. Then, in July, 1850, reports of a slight insurrection in Cuba reached America. Two weeks later, against Fillmore's injunction, López slipped out of New Orleans with 500 eager volunteers and steamed for Cuba. López's filibusterers were mostly Southerners—restless Mexican War veterans, hot-blooded youths, adventurers and drifters; not more than 15 of them were Cubans.

The invaders landed at Playtas, about 60 miles from Havana, and moved inland. But the mass of Cubans did not revolt as predicted, and within two days 50 Americans, including the Attorney General's nephew, were captured by the Spanish. They promptly were executed by firing squads. A few days later, Spanish troops surrounded and captured the rest of the expedition. López was publicly garroted in Havana; the other 162 survivors were shipped to Spain to work in the silver mines. So ended López's filibuster. A century later another American-sponsored invasion of Cuba would fail similarly, on the beaches of the "Bay of Pigs."

American reaction to the executions was strong. Expansionists called for government intervention, patriots urged retaliation; in New Orleans rioters destroyed the Spanish consulate. Fillmore, however, was like the eye of a tornado; as the winds of passion swirled around him, he maintained his composure and common sense. In an act of political courage, he publicly censured the filibusterers and admitted Spain's right to punish the invaders as she had. Then he negotiated for the return of the American prisoners sent to Spain, agreeing to a $25,000 indemnity for their release. (This was considerably cheaper than the $50 million in food and drugs which Castro received in 1963 for the 1,000-odd captured Cuban exiles.)

Fillmore's coolness under pressure averted a possible international conflict and a probable domestic crisis. Any effort by the United States to annex Cuba would have involved Spain, of course, and France and England, which had interests in the Caribbean. But more important, the acquisition of Cuba, said the President in his annual message to Congress, might have revived "those conflicts of opinion between the different sections of the country which lately shook the Union to its center."

It is one of the ironies of politics that Fillmore was able to save the country but not himself. When he sought the Whig presidential nomination in 1852, he lost out to General Winfield Scott on the 53rd ballot, 159 to 112. His diligent execution of the Fugitive Slave Law had cost him vital northern Whig support. As one Northerner wrote: "We can rally on a man pledged to *let the Compromise alone,* but not for one who figured in the enactment of the Fugitive law."

Scott, a pompous nonentity, was decisively beaten by Democrat Franklin Pierce. His defeat marked the disintegration of the Whig coalition. By 1854 the various Whig factions had been absorbed into the Democratic Party, the new Republican Party and the American (Know-Nothing) Party.

On March 4, 1853, Fillmore handed over the reins of government to Franklin Pierce. It was a raw, damp day, and Mrs. Fillmore became chilled and caught pneumonia. She died shortly afterward, and a grief-stricken Fillmore retired to Buffalo and private life with his two children, Millard, Jr., twenty-four, and Mary, twenty.

In 1856 he returned to politics to run for President on the American Party ticket. The party platform called for the exclusion of foreigners and Catholics from public office and for a 21-year residence for immigrants as qualification for citizenship. Fillmore's candidacy was a bad idea gone wrong. He finished a poor third in the balloting, behind Democrat James Buchanan and Republican John Frémont. When the former President saw the results, he confided to a friend, "I consider my political career at an end, and have nothing more to ask." Two years later he married an attractive, wealthy widow, and until his death in 1874 he lived in Buffalo in the comfort and dignity he always had sought.

Fillmore often is dismissed as a vain man and a mediocre President. These judgments derive mainly from the *Autobiography* of Thurlow Weed, Fillmore's principal adversary. Fillmore's actions show something more than Weed was content to record. Certainly there was no vanity in the former President's reply to

Oxford University's offer of an honorary degree. "I had not the advantage of a classical education," he said, "and no man should, in my judgment, accept a degree he cannot read."

As a President, he is underrated. Presiding with reason over a nation racked with passion, he faced the southern challenge of secession and checked the country's slide toward bloodshed. Americans may rejoice, writes historian Allan Nevins, "that the clash of two civilizations was postponed until the North was relatively much stronger. . . ."

Slavery itself proved to be too big an issue for Fillmore, but by 1850 the problem had outgrown most men. Fillmore's immediate successors, Pierce and Buchanan, made no headway with it. It took Abraham Lincoln—and the Union armies—to settle the issue once and for all.

I am tired of such talk. Let them impeach if they want to.

—ANDREW JOHNSON to friends upon his defiance of the Tenure of Office Act

3 Andrew Johnson: 1865

On April 9, 1865, in a farmhouse outside the village of Appomattox Court House, the long battle over slavery ended and the bitter struggle over southern reconstruction began. It is still going on today, more than a century later.

The war had ended, but hatred and madness did not. Five days after Appomattox, a fanatic southern sympathizer who believed he was "an agent of the Lord" stole into the presidential box at Ford's Theatre as easily as he might have walked through a revolving door, and shot Abraham Lincoln. It was the first assassination of an American President.

Lincoln's successor, Vice-President Andrew Johnson, was asleep at the Kirkwood House, a few blocks away from the theatre. He had retired early, declining a friend's invitation to join him at the play. Johnson had no time for such "frivolity" as plays. Once he had attended a vaudeville show in Baltimore, where he had been delighted by "48 little girls . . . performing every imaginable evolution." But he preferred to read and study, and besides, in the morning he was leaving for his home in Tennessee. With the Senate not scheduled to convene until December, there was, as usual, literally nothing for the Vice-President to do in Washington.

His friend raced back to the Kirkwood House to tell Johnson the news. Secretary of State William Seward also had been attacked. It was learned later that the Vice-President had been marked for assassination, too. But the conspirator assigned to the task had lost his nerve.

The Vice-President asked his friend to "go to the President and Seward, see them personally," and report back to him. A few hours later he listened to the report with lowered eyes. Lincoln still lingered, but he was unconscious and had no chance to live; Seward, slashed and bleeding, was in critical condition. Outside, a cold rain whipped through the streets.

Johnson slipped into a coat, slouched his hat over his eyes and went to see the dying President. He waved aside a suggestion that a detachment of troops escort him. The Vice-President was absolutely fearless. He was not tall, only a stocky five-foot-eight, but his deep-set black eyes and rugged features gave him a formidable appearance. Johnson was a man, reported novelist Charles Dickens after meeting him, "who would have to be killed to be got out of the way."

Many had threatened to do so. In one campaign, Tennessee Know-Nothings warned Johnson—who had described the typical Know-Nothing as "a loathsome reptile"—not to make a speech scheduled in their district. He showed up anyway—armed with a pistol.

He placed the pistol in view. "I have been informed," he told the hostile audience, "that part of the business to be transacted on the present occasion is the assassination of the individual who now has the honor of addressing you. I suppose therefore that this is the first business in order. If any man has come here today for this purpose this is the proper time to proceed."

With his right hand on his pistol, Johnson paused to survey the crowd. Nobody stirred. "Gentlemen, it appears that I have been misinformed," he said, and gave his speech, which included a strong denunciation of Know-Nothing intolerance.

It was 2 A.M. when Johnson reached the President's bedside. Less than 12 hours previously, the two men had talked privately. Johnson had been Lincoln's own choice for Vice-President. A Democrat from the "border" state of Tennessee, Johnson had balanced the 1864 Republican (or "National Union") ticket, replacing Lincoln's first-term Vice-President, Hannibal Hamlin of Maine. As usual, the choice had been dictated by political expediency. The fact that Johnson had executive experience as well as expedient affiliations had been a minimal consideration in his nomination; he had not been expected to execute. So it is in politics: the pursuit of victory obscures the lessons of the past.

After a 30-minute deathwatch, the Vice-President

returned to the Kirkwood House. That morning, at 7:22, Lincoln died. Less than three hours later, Andrew Johnson, who had started in life as a tailor's apprentice, took the oath as the 17th President of the United States.

He was fifty-seven years old. As he stood in the parlor of the Kirkwood House, surrounded by most of Lincoln's Cabinet, a few Senators and friends, he may have thought that but for the terrible events of the past night he now would be on his way to Tennessee. Instead he was President. Chief Justice Salmon P. Chase, after administering the oath of office, extended his hand to the new President in "sad congratulations."

A brief statement was in order. "Gentlemen," Johnson began, "I must be permitted to say that I have been almost overwhelmed by the announcement of the sad event which has so recently ocurred. . . ."

It was his only reference to his predecessor. The incredibility of his present position turned his thoughts, not surprisingly, toward himself. Senator James G. Blaine noted that "a boundless egotism was inferred from the line of his remarks" by those present. But it was not vanity. Johnson was not a vain but a self-made man, which makes of self-esteem a kind of self-defense. "My nature," he once admitted, "is rather defensive in character." He was, indeed, defensive, and he was fearless and stubborn, as Dickens correctly noted; and all these qualities would shape his presidency in the struggle over reconstruction.

". . . I have long labored to ameliorate and alleviate the condition of the great mass of the American people," he continued in the crowded Kirkwood House. "Toil and an honest advocacy of the great principles of free government have been my lot. Duties have been mine, consequences are God's."

It was true, if overstated. From the beginning Johnson's life had been one of toil and duty. In Raleigh, North Carolina, where he was born, there were only three classes of people: rich whites, poor whites and Negroes. Johnson's family was poor. When he was only three, his father, "an honest man, loved and respected by all who knew him," died from exposure suffered in pulling two drowning men from an icy stream. The family went from poor to indigent.

At the age of fourteen Johnson was bound to James J. Selby to learn the tailor's trade. He learned his trade well. "I always gave a snug fit," he quipped once when someone spoke scornfully about his tailoring background, and even when he was President, he couldn't resist ducking into a tailor's establishment to exchange shop talk. The first time he returned to Raleigh as President, he subtly alluded to his former trade. "I have no other ambition in life," he said in his speech to a huge welcoming crowd, "but to mend and repair the breaches in the torn and tattered Constitution of my country."

"Bless his dear heart," cried an old lady who had mistaken *breaches* for *breeches,* "Andy's goin' to come back home and open up his tailor shop again!"

He had run away from Raleigh and Selby when he was sixteen, to escape "persecution" at the hands of an old woman whose house he and three other bound boys had stoned, probably as a prank. When he drifted back a year later he had behind him the experience of two tailor shops of his own. But Raleigh was not for him, so in the summer of 1826, he and his older brother, mother and stepfather tossed their meager belongings into a two-wheeled pony cart and headed for the hill country of East Tennessee to seek a fresh start.

The family settled in Greeneville, a small town in a fertile valley nestled among the Cumberland Mountains to the west and the lofty Blue Ridge to the east and north. Within a few months Johnson had his own tailor shop and a pretty young wife, the former Eliza McCardle.

As Mrs. Fillmore had done in Buffalo, the new Mrs. Johnson took into her own hands the education of her husband. Johnson could spell a little and read simple words, but he could not write. He never had been to school. His only education had been gleaned from *The American Speaker,* a popular collection of speeches and essays which had been given to him while he was at Selby's in Raleigh. Johnson's wife tutored him well. Within a few years he was writing legibly and reading everything he could lay his hands on, from Aesop's *Fables* to Plutarch's *Lives.* And while he worked at the tailor's bench, measuring customers and snipping and sewing cloth, he paid a man 50 cents a day to read to him aloud.

Mrs. Johnson retained a strong influence over her husband throughout the 48 years of their marriage. She looked after his business affairs as they gradually improved, ran the household and raised three sons and two daughters. "Andrew, Andrew," she would say softly when Johnson lost his temper, and instantly his anger would subside. She was an invalid during the presidential years, and her daughters, Martha and Mary, took her place as official White House hostess. They also were close to their father. "I shouldn't wonder," says one historian, "if Andrew Johnson did not consult his wife and daughters more than he did any fellow statesman." Mrs. Johnson survived her husband's death in 1875 by only a few months.

Johnson worked and studied long hours, but he never was too busy to discuss politics, and the one-room frame workshop of "A. Johnson, Tailor" quickly became a political center. In 1828 Johnson himself ran for office as a Jacksonian Democrat and champion of the workingman. He was elected alderman of Greeneville. In the next 15 years he served again as alderman, as Mayor of Greeneville (three terms) and in the state legislature and Senate. People began calling him "the new Andy Jackson."

In 1842 he won a seat in Congress. Congressman Johnson was for slavery—he now kept a few slaves himself—*and* the Union. "Congress has no power to interfere with the subject of slavery," he said in 1850. At the same time, he placed "the Constitution and the Union above the objects for which the Union was formed." This division of his loyalties, and his working-class background, brought down upon him the scorn of Jefferson Davis and the southern planters in Congress.

Johnson served five terms in Congress. He fought for a Homestead bill which would provide free public land to people who would settle it, and he opposed high tariffs, public debt and government waste. Every two years he took to the stump and talked his opponent to defeat. A New York newspaper correspondent, describing Johnson's style, wrote that "he cut and slashed right and left . . . he tore big wounds and left something behind to fester and be remembered." Later, at the presidential level, these tactics would prove disastrous. But in the 1840's and 1850's, in wide-open Tennessee, they proved so effective that, in 1853, the Whig-controlled legislature, as a last resort, "gerrymandered"—the word dates back to 1812 when Massachusetts Governor Elbridge Gerry had the boundaries of an election district redrawn to his advantage;

the new district was shaped like a salamander—Johnson out of Congress.

Johnson, undismayed, ran for Governor of Tennessee and won two terms. From the governorship he vaulted to the United States Senate in 1857.

It was a time of crisis, in the nation and in the Senate. The Compromise of 1850 was wearing thin. Northerners refused to comply with the hated Fugitive Slave Laws; Southerners agitated for protection of their "property." Johnson, trying desperately to secure passage of a Homestead bill, was caught in the swirl of the slavery dispute. The Dred Scott decision, fighting over slavery in Kansas, John Brown's raid, Jefferson Davis's Senate resolutions—all these deepened the sectional crises to the point that, in 1860, southern extremists threatened secession if Lincoln were elected President.

On election eve Johnson was in Tennessee conferring with friends. He had campaigned halfheartedly for Breckenridge, the southern Democratic candidate, but he saw that Lincoln would be elected and that "the South would seize upon his election as a pretext to secede." Johnson was opposed more to secession than to slavery, and he saw that one would not survive the other. A state does not have the right to secede, he told his secessionist host. "When the crisis comes," he added solemnly, "I will be found standing by the Union."

And so he was. On December 20, 1860, South Carolina seceded from the Union. Within six weeks, seven other states followed suit. President Buchanan, in despair, wrung his hands and waited for President-elect Lincoln to assume the responsibility for acting. Lincoln's conciliatory speeches proved futile. One by one the southern Senators and Representatives resigned their seats in Washington to take their places in the new Confederacy. But not Johnson. "I am opposed to secession," he stated in a Senate speech. "I am in the Union and intend to stay in it." He was the only southern Senator to remain loyal to the United States.

When Tennessee seceded, Johnson was in the state stumping against secession. The secessionists marked him for death. Secretly, he left his family and escaped to Washington. Thirteen thousand mountaineers, loyal to Johnson, eventually followed his path to the Union ranks.

What had made Johnson a traitor to the South made him a hero to the North, and Lincoln welcomed his presence in the Senate. He gave Johnson an important voice in the conduct of the Tennessee military campaign, and when General Grant drove the Confederate forces from around Nashville in 1862, the President appointed Johnson Military Governor of the state.

Johnson resigned from the Senate to take the post. It was a dangerous assignment. Confederate armies still held East Tennessee and threatened Nashville. In fact, a few months after Johnson's arrival, the Confederates surrounded and attacked the state capital. Three times the military defenders prepared to evacuate the city. Johnson, watching the shifting battle lines on the outskirts of the city from the cupola of the capitol building, refused to concede defeat. "I am no military man," he declared, "but anyone who talks of surrender I will shoot." Nashville held out.

As Military Governor, Johnson had complete executive, legislative and judicial authority, and he exercised it. He decreed laws, levied taxes, censored the press and jailed disloyal public officials. It was a difficult job. Tennessee was ravaged by war and its citizens were divided in loyalties; Johnson's own wife and youngest son were ill with tuberculosis. "My mind is tortured and my body exhausted," he wrote his wife in 1862. "Sometimes I feel like giving all up in despair." Yet, by 1865, Tennessee had a Unionist government, and Johnson himself was Vice-President. He was preparing to help Tennessee show the rest of the South the way to reconstruction. Then, suddenly, he was President, intoning a solemn "inaugural" in the parlor of the Kirkwood House. Yes, his life had been hard. But the worse was yet to come.

The same day that Johnson took the oath as President the radical Republicans met in caucus to consider "the necessity of a new Cabinet and a new line of policy less conciliatory than that of Mr. Lincoln." Leader of the radicals was seventy-three-year-old Pennsylvania Congressman Thaddeus Stevens. A thin-lipped, sharp-tongued autocrat with a passion for gambling, ladies and civil rights, he was the ablest man in Congress. His counterpart in the Senate was Bostonian Charles Sumner, a dedicated reformer who had espoused the cause of world peace, women's suffrage, temperance and abolitionism. Sumner was fastidious to the point of vanity. A friend once remarked to General Grant that Sumner put no faith in the Bible.

"No, he didn't write it," Grant replied, in one of his rare flashes of wit.

The consensus of the radicals was that the new President, unlike the old one, would cooperate with them in reconstruction. That evening radical Senator Benjamin F. Wade of Ohio told the President, "Johnson, we have faith in you. By the gods, there will be no trouble now in running the government."

Johnson smiled and repeated what he often had said in the past: "Treason must be made infamous and traitors must be impoverished." It was the last time the two men were to agree.

Six weeks later, on May 29th, Johnson revealed his reconstruction policy in two proclamations. One granted amnesty to Southerners—with some exceptions —who took an oath of allegiance to the United States. The other outlined the pattern for executive recognition of Confederate state governments: abolition of slavery, voiding of ordinances of secession and repudiation of war debts.

Johnson's program was almost as lenient as Lincoln's initial plan, which the radicals had denounced. It was, as Johnson himself admitted, "restoration," not reconstruction. The radicals were both angry and bewildered; they had convinced themselves that Johnson was one of them. "Is there no way," Stevens asked Sumner, "to arrest the insane course of the President in reconstruction?" Sumner wrote to Wade: "I do not understand the Presdt." Wade thought "the extravagant eulogisms of Mr. Lincoln" had induced Johnson "to become the feeble copyish [sic] of a very feeble original."

But Johnson simply was being Johnson. "I was born a states-rights Democrat and I shall die one," he once said. That tells more about Johnson's presidency than volumes of commentary.

Between Johnson and the radicals the principal issue was what to do with four million suddenly freed Negroes. The radicals wanted to remodel southern society and guarantee to the Negro not only freedom but equal rights. "Every man," said Stevens, "no matter what his race or color . . . has an equal right to justice, honesty and fair play with every other man; and the law should secure him those rights." Johnson, like most men of his time, both North and South, believed the Negro was inferior to the white man. Still, he personally favored "giving protection to all freedmen . . . in person and property without regard to color." Under his program, however, the southern states were not obliged to protect the Negro's civil rights. They had to accept only emancipation. Johnson also suggested that the states give the ballot "to colored soldiers, to the more intelligent Negroes, and to those owning $300 of property"—advice which was ignored completely. In any case the radicals wanted more. "If all whites must vote, then must all blacks," insisted Sumner.

But Johnson considered voting qualifications and civil rights matters of *state* jurisdiction and not subject to federal legislation or even to executive fiat. He was not much concerned over the question of executive vs. congressional reconstruction. His state papers indicate that he was willing to let Congress reconstruct the South *so long as Congress included among its member-*

ship the southern states' Representatives, which he insisted had been elected validly under his restoration program; that way the southern states would have a voice in their fate. Johnson believed that the Southerner, left to his own devices, gradually would grant the Negro justice. In that, history proved him wrong.

Meanwhile, the southern states, under Johnson's program, organized governments and elected Representatives—mostly former Confederate officials—to Congress. They also enacted so-called "Black Codes," laws of "vagrancy" and "apprenticeship" which tied the Negro to the land as effectively as slavery had done. These codes aroused the wrath of Northerners, radicals and moderates alike. But Johnson, although he was annoyed by the passage of the codes, rationalized them as "essential" to the "comfort, protection and security" of the Negro.

"Among all the leading Union men of the North . . ." Stevens wrote to Johnson, "I do not find one who approves of your policy. . . . Can you not hold your hand and wait the action of Congress?" It was the second time in a month that Stevens had approached the President. Johnson failed to acknowledge either letter. Instead he went before Congress in December and declared the nation reunited and restoration virtually completed.

He had worked hard at it. A typical day for him began at six A.M. and lasted until midnight. From seven to ten he usually read or wrote on a tall stand-up desk in his office. At ten he received the public— mostly Southerners petitioning for pardon. When the President's office was thrown open, one observer noted, a "strong tide instantly set towards it, resulting in a violent jam at the door." Lunch was at eleven, after which Johnson received distinguished callers, then the general public again. At three he strolled around the White House grounds, if he could get away from his office; usually he couldn't. Dinner was at seven. At eight he retired to the library with a pet cat and a pot of coffee, to read and study.

"The Grim Presence" one of his secretaries called Johnson. That was his official face; in private life he was warm and tender. He loved children and animals. His grandchildren were given the run of the White House, and sometimes they burst into his office and dragged him off to play on the lawn. He found mice in his bedroom and placed a basket of grain there to feed them. Having gained, as he put it, "the confidence of the little creatures," he sprinkled the hearth with water so they could wash down their food!

"He wanted to do all the work of the executive himself," the same secretary observed. The radicals felt he was doing the work of Congress as well. Now they fought back. When the 39th Congress convened in December, Stevens instructed the Clerk of the House to omit the names of southern Representatives-elect—most of whom were Democrats—when he called the roll. Without such recognition, the Southerners could not take their seats in Congress; and a state without congressional representation could not be considered in the Union. It was a brilliant parliamentary maneuver. In one stroke it nullified Johnson's entire restoration program.

Stevens next step was to place reconstruction under

congressional jurisdiction. He organized a Joint Committee on Reconstruction—nine Representatives and six Senators "who shall inquire into the condition of the States which formed the so-called Confederate States of America, and report whether they, or any of them, are entitled to be represented in either House of Congress. . . ." The Committee, of course, was dominated by radicals and controlled by Stevens himself.

So was presented to Johnson the great political challenge of his presidency. At this point victory still hung in the balance, for Congress was not united against the President. Republicans outnumbered Democrats in both houses of Congress, 141 to 43 in the House and 39 to 11 in the Senate.* But the Republicans, who in economic issues were uniformly "conservative," were split on the issue of reconstruction into "radical," "moderate" and "administration" factions. The moderates were the largest group and held the balance of power. These were the men whose support Johnson had to win if he were going to influence reconstruction.

The test was not long in coming. In February, 1866, Congress passed a bill giving the Freedmen's Bureau (a wartime agency created to assist destitute Negroes—and whites—with emergency food, clothing and shelter) jurisdiction over alleged civil rights viola-

---

*Had the southern Representatives-elect been seated, the Republican majorities would have been reduced from 98 to about 40 in the House and from 28 to about 6 in the Senate. This is one reason the Republicans —moderates as well as radicals—denied the Southerners their seats. They hoped to use Negro suffrage to replace these southern Democrats with reconstruction Republicans and therefore consolidate Republican political power.

tions. Johnson vetoed the measure on the grounds that the southern states had not been represented in the consideration of legislation which affected them. His veto was sustained in the Senate by two votes—the only Johnson veto to stand up in Congress.

Johnson had won the battle but lost the war, for the veto cost him vital moderate support. When he vetoed a civil rights bill in April, citing among his other reasons that it operated "in favor of the colored and against the white race," Congress promptly passed the measure over his objections. In June Congress voted for the 14th Amendment (which made the Negro a citizen), despite Johnson's opposition to it on the grounds of states' rights and because it barred from office former Confederate officials, pardoned or not. That same month the Joint Committee ruled that the southern states (which also opposed the 14th Amendment) were not entitled to congressional representation. Then, a few days later, Congress passed a revised Freedmen's Bureau bill over Johnson's veto. The radicals, with moderate support, assumed command of reconstruction.

Having failed to win the support of the moderates, Johnson looked directly to the voters for vindication. The mid-term congressional elections were due in November. In late August Johnson began his famous 2,000-mile "swing around the circle," in which he spoke in virtually every large city, and countless small towns, east of the Mississippi. It was the first large-scale "whistle-stop" campaign by an American President.

Radical sympathizers heckled and baited the President along the way. On several occasions Johnson lost his temper and exchanged insults with his tormentors, as he had done when stumping in Tennessee. Seward, commenting on the exchanges, remarked to Secretary of the Navy Gideon Welles that Johnson was "the best stumper in America." Welles replied that the President should not be a stumper at all.

It didn't make much difference. In November the radicals captured two-thirds of each house in a landslide victory. Radical propaganda, northern campaign contributions, the veterans' vote and even the President's intemperate stumping were blamed for Johnson's defeat. They all were factors, but the central factor, says historian Kenneth M. Stampp, was the northern voters' "genuine fear that President Johnson, through his southern governments, was going to lose the peace. . . ." Johnson never did understand this fear.

Now the radicals could do as they pleased, and they did. Within 18 months they passed four Reconstruction Acts dividing the South into five military districts subject to martial law. The Negro was given the ballot—703,000 Negroes and 627,000 whites were registered—and southern ratification of the 14th Amendment became mandatory.

Johnson vetoed each measure, and Congress quickly passed each one again over his objections. The President, however, conscientiously executed each of these laws, and that was to prove important later.

Meanwhile, the radicals began an assault on the presidency itself. In July, 1866, they had pushed through a bill preventing the President from appointing new Supreme Court justices. On March 2, 1867,

Congress virtually stripped the President of the command of the army by legislation requiring him to issue all military orders through the General of the Army (Grant). The same day Congress passed the Tenure of Office Act, which prohibited the President from removing, without Senate consent, any official who had been appointed "by and with the advice and consent of the Senate." This was designed to prevent Johnson from making any Cabinet changes, especially in the War Department, where Stanton was functioning as a radical ally.

Johnson vetoed all these measures, of course—to no avail. The Tenure of Office Act was especially galling to him. Stanton, who had served Lincoln brilliantly and loyally, had turned his talents to subverting Johnson's administration. He was a strange man, great in war and mean in dispute. "No man of a proper sense of honor," he declared in a Cabinet meeting, "would remain in the Cabinet when invited to resign." But he chose to ignore Johnson's pointed hint that the Secretary should take his own advice.

Johnson tolerated him—which was a serious mistake. Then in August he learned that Stanton had authored a section of the third Reconstruction Act, and he sent him the following note:

SIR: Public considerations of a high character constrain me to say that your resignation as Secretary of War will be accepted.

Very respectfully yours,
ANDREW JOHNSON

The Senate was not then in session, and Stanton declined to resign "before the next meeting of Congress" in December. Johnson suspended Stanton from office and appointed Grant Secretary of War *ad interim*. To this Stanton submitted "under protest." "The turning point has at last come," Johnson said. "The Rubicon is crossed."

To no one's surprise the Senate did not concur in Stanton's dismissal. Grant, informed of the Senate's decision, turned the War Department back over to Stanton. For the first time a President was forced to retain as a confidential adviser a man whom he distrusted and disliked.

Johnson had hoped that Grant would resist Stanton's reinstatement and so force the issue of the constitutionality of the Tenure of Office Act to the Supreme Court. But Grant, with his eye on the 1868 presidential nomination, had played it safe. Now Johnson, faced with the choice of defying the Senate or submitting to it, chose defiance. His friends advised him to drop the matter; talk of impeachment was in the air. But Johnson would not be intimidated. "I am tired of such talk," he told his friends. "Let them impeach if they want to." On February 21, 1868, he dismissed Stanton and so informed the Senate.

The next day the radicals moved to impeach him. On February 24th impeachment on 11 charges was carried by a straight party vote, 126 to 47. The official charge cited as Johnson's "high crimes and misdemeanors" violation of the Tenure of Office Act, alleged violation of the Command of the Army Act and alleged "ridicule" of Congress. It was a weak case at best. Johnson had executed faithfully even those laws which he had vetoed. He had defied the Tenure of Office Act, but only to test its constitutionality; this was no "high crime" nor "misdemeanor."

There was no case even for legislative expediency. Congress had no trouble passing legislation over Johnson's vetoes, and anyway, only a few months of his term remained. The fact is that any ideals that may have motivated the radicals in their reconstruction policies were absent in their impeachment of the President. Behind the legal abstractions of the impeachment articles lay the radicals' real purposes: to purge Johnson and render the presidency itself impotent before the will of Congress.

On March 5th, the case went to the Senate for trial. This in itself was a travesty of justice. The Senate was asked to judge a man for alleged violations of laws which the Senate had passed. And, if the Senate found the President guilty, he would be succeeded by Ben Wade, President pro tempore of the Senate. Finally, to cap this Alice-in-Wonderland situation, the Senate ruled that Senator Wade could participate in the judging—in effect, vote himself into the White House!

This flaw in the impeachment process was eliminated in 1886, when Congress passed a law making Cabinet members, in order of their rank, next in line for the presidency after the Vice-President. This put the Secretary of State, an appointed official, third in the presidential succession. In 1947, Congress returned the succession to elected officials, first the Speaker of the House, then the President pro tempore of the Senate, and *then* the Cabinet officers in order of their rank. So the absurd situation of 1868 is not likely to recur.

Chief Justice Chase presided over Johnson's trial. The President's lawyers, five of the best legal men in the country led by Attorney General Henry Stanbery, asked for 40 days to reply to the charges; the Senate gave them 10. They prepared a brilliant defense of the President. Johnson himself never appeared at the trial. His lawyers decided the volatile President could only hurt, not help, his case.

Only the firm hand of Chief Justice Chase—himself a radical—prevented the radicals from turning the trial into a political inquisition. Forty-one witnesses appeared; countless documents were read. The radicals took turns haranguing against the President, Stevens, slowly dying, left the management of the House case to General B. F. Butler, a political opportunist of whom a fellow Republican later said, when a Democratic tide had swept Butler and the rest of the Republicans out of office, "Butler defeated, everything else lost."

In the White House, Johnson waited. He worked regularly, argued with his lawyers, granted interviews to sympathetic reporters and read books about martyrs. By May 16th the Senate was ready to vote on the 11th charge, the one the radicals considered most likely to get the necessary two-thirds vote for conviction.

The President needed 19 of 54 votes for acquittal. He was sure of the votes of the 12 Democrats and reasonably sure of the votes of 6 Republicans. The one uncertain vote was that of Senator Edmund Ross of Kansas. Ross was a radical, but he had refused to commit himself to a guilty vote, despite intense radical pressure and even a $20,000 bribe. As the Clerk intoned the 11th Article of Impeachment, no one in the hushed, crowded Senate chamber knew how Edmund Ross would vote.

After the charge was read, Chief Justice Chase signaled to the Clerk to call the Senate roll.

"Mr. Anthony," the Clerk called. Senator Henry B. Anthony of Rhode Island rose.

"Mr. Anthony," the Chief Justice said, "how say you? Is the respondent, Andrew Johnson, President of the United States, guilty or not guilty of a high misdemeanor as charged in this article?"

"Guilty," answered Senator Anthony.

The roll call continued: two "Not guilties," eight "Guilties," three more "Not guilties," three more "Guilties." . . . By the time Ross's name came up, 14 votes for acquittal had been cast. Four more were almost certain. Everything depended on Ross, who nervously was tearing the paper on his desk into strips.

"Mr. Ross," the Clerk called. Ross rose and some shredded paper on his lap fluttered noiselessly to the floor.

"Mr. Ross," the Chief Justice asked breathlessly, unable to keep the tension out of his voice, "how say you?"

"Not guilty," Ross said.

It was all over. The final vote was 19 to 35 for impeachment, one vote short of the two-thirds necessary for conviction. A White House guard, when he told Johnson the verdict, noted tears rolling down the President's face.

Several days later the Senate voted upon the second and third impeachment charges, but the votes fell as they had on the first ballot and the Senate, convinced that further voting was pointless, adjourned as a court.

The assault on the presidency had been halted. It never again reached such a pitch nor came so close to success. As historian Howard K. Beale says, "Only Johnson's tenacity . . . prevented the establishment of a parliamentary system with Congress omnipotent in Washington where checks and balances had been scrapped."

He preserved the presidency as he never had used it. If a President's job is to persuade, then Johnson must be ranked a failure. He was inflexible at a time when yielding here, forcing there, was necessary. And he violated a basic principle of political leadership by risking his prestige before it was firmly enough established to survive possible defeat.

History has proven that in the issues of reconstruction the radicals were more right than wrong. They sought basically what Americans of good conscience seek today—protection of the Negro's civil and voting rights. Had Johnson preserved his influence over the radicals, he might have exerted the moral and political weight of his office in the formulation of reconstruction policy. As a Southerner who had won the affection and trust of Northerners, he was in a unique position to mediate between North and South. But he misread the North's mood and the South's intentions and, on narrow constitutional grounds, argued for a restored South in which the Negro would be only theoretically free.

His failure cannot be charged to inexperience. He had more executive experience (as Governor of Tennessee) than either Tyler or Fillmore. But, as Richard E. Neustadt says, "mere experience, however relevant, is no assurance that a President will find the confidence he needs just when he needs it most. . . . The power-seeker whose self-confidence requires quick returns and sure success might make a mess of everything, including his own power."

Johnson had no hope of succeeding himself. He did draw 65 votes, the second highest total, on the first ballot at the *Democratic* convention, but he soon dropped out of the running there, too. The Republicans unanimously nominated General Grant.

Seven years later, in March, 1875, Johnson returned to the Senate. He was received with the affection and emotion which the Senate reserves for one of its own on nostalgic occasions. It was Johnson's last triumph. A few months later, during the summer recess, he died of a stroke. He was buried in Greeneville, a copy of the Constitution under his head.

Oh, no, it cannot be true.

—CHESTER A. ARTHUR on learning of President Garfield's death

4 Chester A. Arthur: 1881

The fledgling Republican Party continued to rule the nation against all odds. Grant, despite his incompetence, won two terms as President. He was followed in 1876 by Rutherford B. Hayes. Hayes ran 250,000 votes behind his Democratic opponent, Samuel J. Tilden. But, not to be outdone by the swindlers under Grant, he bought the presidency from southern electors in return for the removal of federal troops from the South, ending radical reconstruction. *Quid pro quo*— something for you and, in exchange, something for me; it was politics as usual.

However, the Republicans named no more Democrats as candidates for Vice-President. A safe radical served with Grant in each of his administrations, and in 1876 William A. Wheeler, a "discreet" New York Republican, was chosen to run with Hayes. Wheeler's qualifications as a potential President may be guessed by Hayes' reaction to him. "And who is William A.

Wheeler?" he asked when he was informed of the convention's choice. Nobody cared. Four years later the party would show the same indifference in naming a candidate for Vice-President. But this time destiny would make the choice significant.

The Republicans convened in Chicago in June, 1880, badly divided on a presidential candidate. Hayes, the incumbent, had committed himself to a single term, so the nomination was up for grabs. Grant, seeking an unprecedented third term, was backed by the "Stalwart" faction of the party, the hard core of professional politicians led by waspish Roscoe Conkling of New York. They wanted control of the executive patronage, which Grant in the past had distributed so carelessly as to riddle his administrations with corruption and make the spoils system a national issue. James G. Blaine, Speaker of the House and runner-up to Hayes in 1876, represented the "Half-Breeds," Republicans who favored civil service reform which would make some federal appointments dependent upon merit rather than politics.

Grant led in the early balloting. Blaine trailed him closely, and the rest of the delegate strength was scattered among five candidates, with former Senator John Sherman of Ohio, a moderate, commanding the largest bloc. For 35 ballots the convention remained deadlocked. On the 36th roll call, the anti-Grant forces combined to nominate James A. Garfield of Ohio, the man who had placed Sherman's name in nomination. The disgruntled Stalwarts, however, threatened to sit on their hands and do nothing during the election.

To get active cooperation, especially in the crucial state of New York, Garfield's supporters offered the New York Stalwarts the vice-presidency.

General Stewart L. Woodford and Levi Morton, both of New York, were approached for the job. Each one consulted with Conkling. "I hope no sincere friend of mine will accept it," Conkling told Woodford; to Morton he said sarcastically, "If you think the ticket will be elected, if you think you will be happy in the association, accept." Both men declined and no doubt later regretted that they had.

The next man approached was Chester A. Arthur, Conkling's lieutenant in New York party politics. Arthur was a machine politician with white gloves. A tall, handsome, black-eyed man who wore mutton-chop whiskers and fashionable clothes, he had a knack for politics and a taste for refinement. "As a politician," said one of his contemporaries, "he was brainy, thorough, careful and devoted to research and minutiae." At the same time, he enjoyed, as one critic put it, "flowers and wine and food, and slow pacing with a lady on his arm, and a quotation from Thackeray or Dickens."

Under Grant he had served as Collector of Customs for the Port of New York. Hayes, a mild reformer, had fired him for using the Customs House as a grazing ground for Conkling's cronies—himself included. But that didn't discourage the New Yorker's supporters.

Arthur looked for Senator Conkling to get his advice on the offer of the vice-presidency. He found him in the press room of the convention hall, nervously pacing the floor. It was hot and humid, but both men were impeccably dressed, as usual.

"I have been hunting everywhere for you, Senator," Arthur said. "The Ohio men have offered me the vice-presidency."

"Well, sir," Conkling snapped, "you should drop it as you would a red-hot shoe from the forge." He kept pacing the floor, his hands clasped behind his back.

Arthur looked resentful. "I sought you to consult," he said, "not—"

"What is there to consult about?" Conkling interrupted. "This trickster of Mentor [Garfield's farm] will be defeated before the country."

"There is something else to be said," Arthur insisted.

"What, sir, you think of accepting?" Conkling stopped pacing now.

"The office of Vice-President is a greater honor than I ever dreamed of attaining," Arthur replied emphatically. "A barren nomination would be a great honor. In a calmer moment you will look at this differently."

"If you wish for my favor and my respect, you will contemptuously decline it," Conkling said coldly.

Arthur looked the Senator straight in the eye and said, "Senator Conkling, I shall accept the nomination and I shall carry with me the majority of the delegation."

Shortly afterwards the convention nominated Arthur over Elihu B. Washburne of Illinois, 468 to 199. Reaction ran from bad to worse. "The nomination of Arthur is a ridiculous burlesque," John Sherman wrote to a friend, "and I am afraid was inspired by a desire to beat the ticket." Readers of the independent liberal weekly *The Nation* wrote letters to Editor E. L. Godkin asking if they could vote for Garfield without voting for Arthur. Godkin replied that, although "scratching" Arthur was impossible, "there is no place in which his powers of mischief will be so small as in the vice-presidency, and it will remove him during a great part of the year from his own field of activity.

"It is true," Godkin added, "General Garfield, if elected, may die during his term of office, but this is too unlikely a contingency"—Garfield was only forty-nine and in excellent health—"to be worth making extraordinary provisions for." So Arthur was tucked away in the vice-presidency, and Garfield was to be careful not to be hit by a train. This seemed reasonable enough in June, 1880. But life is full of unreason, and a fool may be fatal to it, as Godkin and the nation were to learn.

Garfield won a close election and spent the first four months of his administration fending off office seekers. He had named Blaine Secretary of State, satisfying the Half-Breeds. The Stalwarts now claimed that Garfield had promised to let them name the Secretary of the Treasury, a post which carried a great deal of lucrative patronage. Garfield denied any deal, although he had indeed conferred with the Stalwarts in New York before the election and had led them to expect certain concessions if they contributed to his election. What these concessions were nobody agreed.

Then Garfield appointed William H. Robertson, a Blaine man, as Collector of Customs of the Port of New York. He was unacceptable to Senator Conkling and the Stalwarts, of course. Arthur tried to persuade the President to withdraw the appointment, but Garfield stood fast. We will see, Garfield wrote to a friend, "whether the President is registering clerk of the Senate or the Executive of the United States."

"Garfield," Arthur told a reporter, "has not been square, nor honorable, nor truthful with Conkling. It's a hard thing to say of a President of the United States, but it's only the truth." So stood the relations between the President and his potential successor.

Conkling attempted to block Robertson's confirmation in the Senate. Failing to do so, he resigned from the Senate in protest, confident that the Republican-controlled New York legislature quickly would renominate him and embarass Garfield. But the politicians who for years had swung into line for "Lord Roscoe" suddenly failed to heed his wishes, and the nomination went to another Stalwart. Conkling was never again a political power.

Arthur did his best to aid Conkling, even going up to Albany to lobby for his renomination. On July 1st the New York *Tribune* published a story saying, "The manly figure of the Vice-President of the United States still stands at Albany under a sign which reads: 'Political dickering and other dirty work done here.'" It was Arthur's last day of lobbying. The next morning President Garfield was shot by a frustrated office seeker in Washington's Pennsylvania Station.

The Vice-President was cruising down the Hudson River at the time, returning to New York City from Albany for the weekend. As he stepped onto the pier in New York, he was told of the tragedy. Garfield and Blaine had been on their way to a holiday and as they approached their train a man had stepped from among the crowd and had fired two shots point-blank at the President. The man's name was Charles J. Guiteau, and he insisted that he had shot Garfield to make Arthur President and unite the Republican Party. "I am a Stalwart of the Stalwarts," he cried. "Arthur is President now!'

Arthur was appalled. He, of course, had never heard of Guiteau; no one had. But the man's half-mad declarations inescapably put the Vice-President and all Stalwarts under a cloud, no matter how undeserved. It was as though, on November 22, 1963, Lee Harvey Oswald had declared in Dallas, "I'm a Texan, and Johnson is President now!"

The consensus was that if Arthur sat in the White

House, Conkling would sit behind him and pull the strings. "How fatal a mistake was made at Chicago," wrote one Midwesterner. Sherman expressed his "strong anticipations of the evil to come." An anonymous wit put it more succinctly: "Chet Arthur, President of the United States?" he asked when he heard the news. "Good God!"

He wasn't President yet. Garfield, though seriously wounded, was still alive. Arthur hurried to Washington to meet any emergency. By July 13th the President's physicians saw "manifest" signs of Garfield's "gradual progress toward complete recovery." Arthur secluded himself, first in Washington, then in New York. Meanwhile, with no one at the helm, the government drifted aimlessly.

No one knew what to do. The President clearly was disabled, but Arthur refused to take up the reins of government. And the Constitution was even less helpful in this situation than in the situation of succession by death. In case of the President's "Inability to discharge" his powers and duties, the Constitution states, "the Same shall devolve on the Vice-President." But who was to determine when the President was disabled? The President himself? Neither Garfield nor Woodrow Wilson, when he was paralyzed by a stroke in October, 1919, volunteered any admission of disability. Former President Eisenhower recently revealed that he considered resigning after his stroke in 1957, but at the time, he confided his intentions to "his wife, his son, his doctors and close associates."

Presumably, Vice-President Nixon was not informed, although Eisenhower did write him a letter outlining the conditions under which Nixon might take over the President's duties. But can any Vice-President decide when to invoke a disability clause? He has a vested interest in any such action and is not likely to be impartial. Arthur himself shuddered at the idea of taking the responsibility, especially under the circumstances of a divided party.

Who, then, could determine presidential disability? The Constitution gives to Congress the power to "by Law provide for the Case of Removal, Death, Resignation or Inability," but it wasn't until July 6, 1965, that Congress used it. On that day the Senate voted 68–5 to send a House-approved disability plan to the 50 states for ratification as the 25th Amendment. Under this amendment the Vice-President becomes Acting President if the President notifies Congress in writing that he is "unable to discharge the powers and duties of his office." If the President cannot, or will not, take the initiative in a disability situation, the Vice-President, in concert with a majority of the Cabinet or "such other body as Congress may by law provide" (for example, a commission of private citizens, doctors, psychiatrists, etc.), can advise Congress of a disability and take over as Acting President. The President resumes power when he notifies Congress that the disability no longer exists. If the Vice-President, with a majority of the Cabinet or the "other body," should disagree, the issue would be settled by Congress within

21 days, a one-third minority of both houses being sufficient to restore the President to power.

For Chester Arthur, however, there were no such guidelines. The long, hot summer dragged on and no Cabinet meetings were held, no executive orders came from the President's bedside—only medical bulletins. Then on August 26th Garfield developed serious complications, and his physicians predicted that death was now only a matter of time. The nation waited, the politicians waited, Arthur waited; no one could say where anxiety lay heaviest. Finally, on September 19th, the newsboys in the streets began crying, "Garfield dying! . . . The President is dying!" Arthur, in New York, received a telegram from the Cabinet informing him that the end was near.

He didn't wish to believe it. An astute student of the game of politics, Arthur was reluctant to take on the burdens of its ultimate prize. Late that evening, in the security of the soft summer night, he strolled briefly along the streets of the city to which, almost 30 years previously, he had come to seek his fortune. . . .

He was the son of an Irish-born Baptist minister with abolitionist views and restless feet. Elder Arthur also had a barbed tongue—which may have accounted for his frequent changes of address. On one occasion, as a brother minister concluded a long, tedious talk on his visit to the frontier with the admonition that not any sort of minister would do for the West, Elder Arthur jumped to his feet and shouted, "I never knew before why the brother came back!"

Arthur's birthplace is uncertain. It is listed as Fairfield, Vermont, but it may have been Waterville, a small town about 15 miles away. There is even a story that he was born in Canada (and so ineligible to become President), but this appears to be a political fabrication. He was born in 1830, just a year before Senator William Marcy of New York, in a congressional debate, coined the phrase "to the victor belongs the spoils," which was to play so large a part in Arthur's career.

The boy is father to the man, and as a child Arthur "took good care not to get any . . . dirt on his hands." He attended one of the foremost eastern schools, Union College, where he studied the classics, carved his name in the furniture and earned a Phi Beta Kappa key. At graduation he gave an address on "The Destiny of Genius."

After college he studied law and taught school. In 1853 he came to New York to clerk in the law offices of a family friend, and a year later he was admitted to the New York bar to practice law and was accepted into the firm. One of his first cases involved a Negro lady who had been ejected forcibly from a New York streetcar. Arthur, who had inherited his father's abolitionism, won a $500 judgment for damages from the streetcar company, which also instructed its conductors to allow Negroes to ride unmolested.

At about this time Arthur became involved in the ward politics of the new, antislavery Republican Party. He had been a Whig, but that party had collapsed in 1852 around the candidacy of General Winfield "Fuss

n' Feathers" Scott. In 1856 the young precinct politician campaigned for John C. Frémont. He served
on the 18th Ward Young Men's Frémont Vigilance
Committee and took his place as an inspector of
elections at the polls. "From the start," says one of
Arthur's biographers, "he was an organization man
and a 'worker.'"

Recognition was not long in coming. Arthur was a
"regular," he was congenial and he was attractive; to
such people political power in America is always accessible. In 1860, the Governor appointed Arthur
chief engineer of his military staff. It was purely a
ceremonial position. But the following year the Civil
War broke out and Arthur found himself with a job
to do. He did it well, so well he was appointed Assistant Quartermaster General of New York. Later he
became Quartermaster General, and from then on he
usually was addressed as General Arthur.

As Quartermaster General, Arthur had to shelter
and provision the thousands of troops which were being recruited in New York and which were passing
through the city from New England to the front. He
did it by contracting the feeding, building and supply-
ing to the lowest responsible bidders. It was the kind
of arrangement that abounds in opportunities for graft,
but Arthur left the job poorer than when he had
taken it.

He did a good job. "The secret of [his] success,"
reported the New York *Times,* "was his executive
ability, and his knowledge of men." A mild-mannered
man, Arthur could be tough when he had to be. When

he was Quartermaster General, he discovered that one ragged regiment, dissatisfied with army rations (an old story), was plundering the local restaurants for food. Arthur called the leader of the regiment, "Billy" Wilson, a well-known alderman from the roughest part of the city, to his office and quietly told him to control his ruffians. Wilson, mistaking Arthur's quiet manner for weakness, replied insolently, "Neither you nor the governor has nothing to do with me. I'm a colonel in the U. S. Army, and you've no right to order me."

"You are not a colonel," Arthur said firmly, "and you will not be until you have raised your regiment to its quota of men and received your commission."

"Well, I've got my shoulder straps anyway," Wilson insisted, "and as long as I wear 'em I don't want no orders from any of you fellers."

Arthur rose and walked over to Wilson. "We'll make short work of those shoulder straps," he said and ripped them off and put Wilson under arrest.

After his term as Quartermaster General, Arthur returned to private law practice and, with his political connections in Washington and New York, did quite well. Allying himself with Conkling, he also rose in state politics. By 1872 the New York *Times* could report, "His name very seldom rises to the surface of metropolitan life, and yet, moving like a mighty undercurrent, this man during the last ten years has done more to mold the course of the Republican Party in this state than any other one man in the country."

In 1859, Arthur had married Ellen Lewis Herndon, a southern girl seven years younger than himself. It was a good marriage. The couple had two sons and a daughter; but unhappily, Mrs. Arthur died suddenly of pneumonia in 1880, leaving Arthur despondent. Six months later he accepted the nomination for Vice-President. And now, on an Indian summer evening in 1881, he was on the threshold of the presidency. He had drifted into success, as so many men do, by being in the right place at the right time. "First in ability on the list of second-rate men," the New York *Times* had called him. . . .

Arthur finished his walk and returned to his study, where a few close friends awaited him. No further news had come about the President. In the study, the conversation was sporadic, strained. About midnight the front doorbell rang, silencing everyone in the study as if by signal. The Vice-President, unable to bear the suspense any longer, stepped into the hallway as a servant opened the door.

"The President is dead," a newspaper reporter called to him.

"Oh, no, it cannot be true," Arthur said. "It cannot be. I have heard nothing."

"The dispatch has just been received at the office."

"I hope—my God, I do hope it is a mistake," Arthur said sadly. He returned to the study. "They say he is dead," he told his friends. "A dispatch has been received. . . ." No one spoke. A few minutes later a telegram arrived from the Cabinet confirming the news and advising Arthur to take the oath as President "without delay."

This was done. Justice John R. Brady of the New York Supreme Court was awakened and brought to the house. Someone wrote out the presidential oath on a scrap of paper; Judge Brady read it and handed it to Arthur, who repeated it, becoming the 21st President of the United States.

Three days later he was in Washington, where he took another oath of office and gave a brief inaugural address. "Men may die," the new President said, "but the fabrics of our free institutions remain unshaken." He promised to continue Garfield's policies and asked the aid of "divine guidance and the virtue, patriotism and intelligence of the American people."

Under the circumstances, it wasn't too much to ask. Garfield's assassination, insisted *Harper's Weekly,* had been caused by "the ferocity and insanity of party spirit, bred by the spoils system." *Harper's* voiced the feelings of most Americans when it concluded that "the abolition of the spoils system is now the most essential and important public duty."

It was a duty for which Arthur, by training, was totally unprepared. Indeed, his experience may be said to have molded quite a different sense of duty. But Arthur rose to the occasion and accepted the challenge. In his first message to Congress he declared himself in favor of a Civil Service Act. A year later, with a reluctant Congress still debating Civil Service legislation, Arthur told the legislators that "the people of the country, without distinction of party," wanted action, and "such action should no longer be postponed."

Congress got the message. Within a few weeks the

House and Senate passed the Pendleton Act, and on January 16, 1883, Arthur signed it into law. It created a bipartisan, three-man Civil Service Commission which was empowered to draw up and administer competitive examinations for a selected list of federal offices. The list of officers was limited, but the President could extend it at his discretion. Federal office holders also were protected against assessments for campaign funds and against reprisals for failure to contribute to these funds.

It was not a sweeping reform, but it was a significant one, and Arthur played a crucial role in making it effective. The heart of the Act was the Commission, which was to be appointed by the President with the consent of the Senate. Arthur could have crippled real reform by appointing mediocre or ineffective commissioners. Instead he named three qualified men to the posts, including, as Chief, Dorman B. Eaton, the Secretary of the Civil Service Reform Association. Under Arthur the law was firmly and fairly administered. "Our function cannot be successfully discharged without the constant, firm and friendly support of the President," the Commission later stated. "That support has never failed."

President Arthur surprised almost everyone who had known Vice-President Arthur. From the beginning of his administration, he was his own man. Garfield's Cabinet, of course, after his death, had agreed to "retire" at the new President's convenience. Arthur replaced every officer except Secretary of War Robert T. Lincoln. Most of the new men were Stalwarts, but they were not Conkling men; they were Arthur men. The President vigorously prosecuted the culprits of the so-called "star route" post office frauds, even though the men were high-ranking Republicans. He vetoed the largest Rivers and Harbors Act—"pork barrel" legislation with some fat for everyone—ever voted by Congress, pointedly noting that the bill was "entirely for the benefit of the particular localities in which it is proposed to make the improvements."

These were not the actions of a machine politician. Arthur seems to have decided to live up to the office of President. That he could do so was not surprising, for he had the dignity, the intelligence, the executive ability and the political know-how to be President. He did not have the drive nor the imagination to be a great President; but the times were shallow, and integrity more than greatness filled their need.

As Arthur gained more public respect he drew more private wrath. "Grant was disgruntled, the New York machine exasperated, Blaine and his followers angry and the Ohio retainers of Senator Sherman distinctly cold," writes biographer George Frederick Howe. Conkling, who had called President Hayes "His Fraudulency," began calling President Arthur "His Accidency." "I have but one annoyance with the Administration of President Arthur," Conkling sneered, "and that is, that in contrast with it, the Administration of Hayes becomes respectable, if not heroic."

In some respects, however, Arthur did not change. He continued to lead the life of an epicure, to exercise his cultivated taste. To the White House he brought a French gourmet chef (the John F. Kennedys followed suit in 1960) and the celebrated artist and decorator Louis Comfort Tiffany. The White House, in the words of one visitor, was "full of modern abominations in upholstery and garish gilding." Arthur commissioned Tiffany—whose elegant glasswork still commands high prices—to completely redecorate the executive mansion. "I will not live in a house looking this way," he said and threatened to pay for the renovations himself if Congress refused to appropriate a sum for them.

Arthur also ordered the first elevator and the first indoor plumbing for the White House. He believed in style in every respect. His formal dinners were, in the words of Mrs. Blaine, "extremely elegant, hardly a trace of the old White House taint being perceptible anywhere, the flowers, the damask, the silver, the attendants, all showing the latest style and an abandon in expense and taste."

The President himself usually retired after midnight and rose late, some time after nine. He ate a "continental breakfast" while dressing, then went directly to his office. Twice a week he met with his Cabinet at noon. Late afternoon was reserved for a carriage drive or a horseback ride, and dinner was at seven. Sometimes the President worked in the evenings. But "quite as often," says biographer Howe, he spent his evenings with friends, concluding with an elaborate midnight supper in his private dining room. From this routine the public got the impression that Arthur was an insouciant President, as indeed he was.

To counteract this image, Arthur's secretaries kept a "property basket" filled with official-looking documents; the President, who frequently was late, would carry this basket into his office to "create an appearance of industry."

Arthur liked his job and tried to secure the 1884 Republican nomination on his own. But he had kept his enemies and lost his friends in the party, and Blaine won the nomination on the fourth ballot. Arthur declined to campaign actively for Blaine. The Republican Party chairman, seeking to consult with the President, found him "ill," "engaged," or "not in"; as a result, Democrat Grover Cleveland won New York—and with it the election—by the slender margin of 1,149 votes.

As a matter of fact, Arthur *was* ill. The epicure's life had taken its toll. While at the White House, Arthur gained weight and lost strength. Travel and rest failed to restore his health, and by the time his term as President ended he was chronically indisposed. Two years later, in the spring of 1886, doctors told him that he had Bright's disease (a kidney ailment), and a dangerous cardiac condition. The former President became despondent. "After all," he told a friend, "life is not worth living for, and I might as well give up the struggle for it now as at any other time, and submit to the inevitable." In the fall he died, propped up in bed and with a quiet smile on his face. He was only fifty-six years old.

Arthur was not an illustrious President. Aside from his role in civil service reform, he did little except confound his critics. Yet, as historian Rexford Tugwell writes in *The Enlargement of the Presidency,* "the office of the President was the better for his having occupied it." He was the last Republican for which that could be said until Theodore Roosevelt assumed office in 1901.

While President I have been President, emphatically. . . .

—THEODORE ROOSEVELT to a friend

5 Theodore Roosevelt: 1901

Theodore Roosevelt wanted to be a great writer and became instead President of the United States when McKinley was assassinated. He accepted this shift in destiny with his customary aplomb. "It is a dreadful thing to come into the presidency this way," he said. "But it would be a far worse thing to be morbid about it." Roosevelt was anything but morbid.

"The gift of the gods to Theodore Roosevelt was joy in life," said muckraker Lincoln Steffens, who knew Roosevelt well. Roosevelt's own contribution was energy. "He was full of life," says historian Rexford G. Tugwell, "always on the move, even when he was not going anywhere very much."

He was born in 1858. As a child he was frail and sickly. But, determined to be vigorous and strong, he exercised to develop his "manly" powers. In college he ran track, boxed and wrestled. "I intended to be a middling decent fellow," he said later, "and I did not intend that anyone should laugh at me with impunity because I was decent."

His family was rich and he was privately tutored, then graduated from Harvard. He began to study law. A year later, in 1881, "finding it would not interfere much with my law," he ran for the New York legislature and won. "I have become a 'political hack,' " he told a former classmate. "But don't think I am going into politics after this year."

He was reelected, of course—twice. Then, in 1884, he suffered a double tragedy. On the same day his mother and his young bride of three years died of disease. Roosevelt, his equanimity shattered as it never would be again, left New York to raise cattle in the wild prairies of North Dakota.

The next two years he spent at his ranch on the Little Missouri, writing, hunting, herding cattle and "riding through the lonely rolling prairie and broken lands." The Dakota Territory was still a land of vast silent spaces where "the wild game stared at the passing horseman." In the spring a man might gallop for miles at a stretch over a carpet of prairie roses; in the winter he might be quickly buried by swirling clouds of blinding snow-dust. The prairie had a "curious fascination" for the young New Yorker; dressed in a sombrero, silk neckerchief, fringed buckskin shirt, sealskin chaps and alligator riding boots, he led a "free and hardy life, with horse and with rifle."

In 1886 he returned to New York to run for Mayor. He lost the election but won a second wife, Edith Carow, and the leisure to write. For three years he

studied and wrote history. Then, in 1889, President Harrison appointed him to the U. S. Civil Service Commission. In six years with the Commission, Roosevelt enhanced his reputation as a reformer and completed a four-volume popular history, *The Winning of the West.* "I don't mind work," he told his sister. "The only thing I am afraid of is that by and by I will have nothing to do, and I should hate to have the children grow up and see me with nothing to do."

There was no fear of that happening. In 1895 Roosevelt was appointed Police Commissioner of New York City and asked to sweep corruption out of the Department, a task that may be likened to the one in Lewis Carroll's "The Walrus and the Carpenter":

> "If seven maids with seven mops
>   Swept it for half a year,
> Do you suppose," the Walrus said,
>   "That they could get it clear?"
> "I doubt it," said the Carpenter,
>   And shed a bitter tear.

Roosevelt was hardly more effective, but he made a lot of noise and got plenty of publicity. He always did. "While he is in the neighborhood," one observer noted, "the public can no more look the other way than the small boy can turn his head away from a circus parade." Roosevelt was a master at making headlines. Reporters quoted him because he was outspoken and controversial and therefore newsworthy. And they liked his boyish exuberance and candor. Even his professed irreproachable virtue could be amusing. Lincoln Steffens and Jacob Riis, two reporters who were close to him, once asked Commissioner Roosevelt if he were pointing toward the presidency. Roosevelt leaped to his feet and ran around his desk.

"Don't you dare ask me that," he shouted, his fist clenched and his teeth bared. "Don't you put such ideas into my head." Then he drew both reporters close to him and explained, "Never, never, you must never either of you remind a man at work on a political job that he may be President. It almost always kills him politically." And he added, confidentially, "I must be wanting to be President. Every young man does. But I won't let myself think of it; I must not, because if I do, I will begin to work for it, I'll be careful, calculating, cautious in word and act, and so—I'll beat myself."

President McKinley appointed him Assistant Secretary of the Navy in 1897, and Roosevelt immediately began campaigning for a stronger Navy and "interference" in Cuba. The nation's press and Congress also were crying for action in Cuba, but McKinley resisted their pressure despite the explosion which sank the battleship *Maine* in Havana harbor. "McKinley," said Roosevelt privately, "has no more backbone than a chocolate eclair." The assessment was more apt than Roosevelt knew. In April, 1898, ten weeks after the *Maine* incident, McKinley succumbed to the war fever and provoked Spain into war.

It was, as Secretary of State John Hay wrote Roosevelt, "a splendid little war." The nation gained hegemony in the Caribbean and a foothold in the Pacific;

Admiral Dewey, the hero of Manila Bay, came home to run for President; Colonel Roosevelt, the hero of San Juan Hill, returned to run for Governor of New York. Roosevelt later wrote a book about his part in the Cuban campaign, *The Rough Riders;* the satirist Finley Peter Dunne ("Mr. Dooley") mockingly suggested calling it "Alone in Cubia."

A group of independent reformers was eager to run Roosevelt for Governor. But Roosevelt declined to run as an Independent. "My desire," he told the reformers, "is to achieve results, not merely to issue manifestoes of virtue." Besides, Senator Thomas C. Platt, the Republican boss of New York, already had expressed interest in a Roosevelt candidacy. Platt, who ruled New York State in the interests of the insurance companies, banks and big corporations, had no love for the unpredictable Roosevelt. But the party had been discredited by scandal and Platt saw that war hero Roosevelt was the only Republican who could win. Roosevelt assured Platt that if he were elected he would "try to get on well with the organization." That satisfied Platt and Roosevelt was nominated.

He campaigned vigorously across the state—with the Rough Riders' bugler at his side—and won a narrow victory. Once elected, he did consult Platt on appointments and policy, but as often as not he ignored the boss's advice. With his usual fanfare, he pushed through reforms in corporate taxation and regulation, in civil service and game preservation. He was careful, however, to avoid an open break with Platt. Roosevelt knew where political power ultimately lay.

A year of Roosevelt was as much reform as Platt

could take. Looking for a way out, he suggested that Roosevelt run for Vice-President on McKinley's ticket. McKinley's first-term Vice-President, Garret A. Hobart, had died in office.

Roosevelt was at first cool to the idea. His interest was in the presidency, and for that, the 1904 nomination seemed to be the best bet. He knew that Platt's idea was "to get me out of the state" and he had no desire to be the principal character in a "vice-presidential burial party."

"I would be simply a presiding officer and that I should find a bore," he told Platt. "I would a great deal rather be anything, say professor of history, than Vice-President."

Senator Mark Hanna, McKinley's alter ego and Republican kingmaker, felt the same way about Roosevelt's candidacy, but for different reasons. Hanna didn't want Roosevelt in Washington any more than Platt wanted him in Albany. "Don't any of you realize that there's only one life between that madman and the presidency?" Hanna protested.

McKinley himself had no enthusiasm for Roosevelt, but he refused to "commit the Administration to any candidate," leaving the choice up to the Republican Convention of 1900. Platt and Hanna now began to play a game of political "old maid," Roosevelt being the undesirable card with which the loser would be stuck. One observer quipped that whenever Platt and Hanna met and parted, Hanna carefully searched his pockets to make sure that Platt had not dropped Roosevelt into one of them.

Roosevelt gradually warmed to the idea of the vice-presidency. He was flattered by the genuine enthusiasm of western and anti-Platt Republicans and goaded on by the coolness of "the McKinley people." Also, he was not sure he could be renominated and reelected in New York.

To the end, however, he continued to proclaim his opposition to the nomination, even to his friends and family. That was his style. Perhaps he even believed his own disclaimers. He had a way of persuading himself of his virtue and innocence. But when the convention met in Philadelphia, Roosevelt's instincts took over and he went as a delegate from New York. His appearance galvanized his supporters. With everyone else in traditional summertime straw hats, Roosevelt strode through the hotel lobbies and delegation headquarters in the black Rough Rider-style felt hat in which he had campaigned for Governor in 1898. The effect was predictable. "Gentlemen," said one delegate to his friends, "that's an acceptance hat." And it was.

The Democrats nominated William Jennings Bryan and Adlai E. Stevenson to run against McKinley and Roosevelt. At the age of forty, Bryan already was making his second run for the presidency; in 1896 he had won the nomination with his fiery "Cross of Gold" speech. He was a remarkable speaker. His friends called the glib young Nebraskan the "Boy Orator of the Platte"; his enemies recalled that the shallow, wide Platte River was "six inches deep and six miles wide at the mouth." Roosevelt in 1896 characterized Bryan and his associates as politically "in hearty sympathy with their remote skin-clad ancestors who lived in caves and fought one another with stone-headed axes and ate the mammoth woolly rhinoceros."

Bryan *was* slightly out of tune with the times. In 1896 he campaigned for the free coinage of silver when the supply of gold was increasing rapidly enough to make the use of silver unnecessary. In 1900 he chose to attack American imperialism just as Americans were glorying in their nation's sudden emergence as a global power.

The Republicans smothered Bryan's attacks with paeans to patriotism and promises of prosperity ("the full dinner pail") for four more years. McKinley campaigned from his front porch, as he had in 1896. Roosevelt, however, made nearly 700 speeches in 24 states, trading verbal blows with Bryan. "I am strong as a bull moose," he had told Hanna after the convention, and he seemed determined to prove it. To many Americans the race seemed to be between Bryan and Roosevelt, as indeed, later events proved that it really had been.

Roosevelt's immediate prospects, however, were dim; in the vice-presidency he appeared headed for political oblivion. After the election someone asked Platt if he were going to the inaugural in Washington. "Yes," Platt replied, "I am going down to see Theodore Roosevelt take the veil." Roosevelt himself told a friend, "I do not expect to go any further in politics." Of McKinley he said, "He is perfectly cordial and friendly with me . . . but he does not intend that I shall have any influence of any kind, sort or description in the administration from the top to the bottom." He prepared to use the vice-presidency as an after-school job and asked a judge if he could study law "in New York or here in Oyster Bay, so as to get admitted to the bar before the end of my term as Vice-President?"

All this was nullified by the events of September 6, 1901. On that hot, humid afternoon, Leon Czolgosz, a twenty-eight-year-old anarchist, joined the line of people in the Temple of Music at the Buffalo Pan-American Exposition who were waiting to shake the hand of the President of the United States. When Czolgosz's turn came, he pushed aside McKinley's outstretched hand and, from beneath a handkerchief, fired two .32-caliber bullets into the President's body. McKinley, astonished, fell back. "Don't hurt that man," he said as his assailant was subdued. Then he whispered to his secretary, "My wife—be careful, Cortelyou, how you tell her—oh, be careful."

Eight days later he died, murmuring the words of his favorite hymn, "Nearer my God to Thee . . ." His bullet wound, not fatal in itself, had become fatally gangrenous.

Roosevelt, having been assured earlier by the doctors that the President was "on the high road to recovery," had gone camping in the Adirondacks. On September 13th a guide rode into camp with word of the President's impending death. In a borrowed horse and wagon, Roosevelt rode 50 miles through the night to the nearest railroad station, where he learned that McKinley had died. He boarded a special train to Buffalo, paid his respects to the dead President and took the oath as 26th President of the United States.

"I wish to say," he announced at the conclusion of the ceremony, "that it shall be my aim to continue, absolutely unbroken, the policy of President McKinley for the peace, the prosperity and the honor of our beloved country."

As one wit later said, Roosevelt carried out McKinley's policies—and buried them.

The new President was quick to assert his authority. On his first day at the White House, he assured reporters that he felt "as much a constitutionally elected President" as McKinley. "Due to the act of a madman, I am President," he said, "and shall act in every word and deed precisely as if I and not McKinley had been the candidate for whom the electors cast the vote for President." He already had done that during the campaign.

For the record, Roosevelt assumed an attitude of resignation toward his new responsibilities. "Here is the task, and I have got to do it to the best of my ability, and that is all there is about it," he told his good friend Senator Henry Cabot Lodge. Off the record, however, he displayed more than a stoical sense of duty. Lincoln Steffens, an astute observer, described the succession as "the greatest joy" of Roosevelt's life. "He strode triumphant around among us," Steffens later wrote, "talking and shaking hands, dictating and signing letters, and laughing. . . . He laughed at the rage of Boss Platt and at the tragic disappointment of Mark Hanna. . . . And he laughed with glee at the power and place that had come to him."

That power—presidential power—had lain dormant

for a decade. The real power in the Republican Party flowed—with the money—from such businessmen as John D. Rockefeller (oil), J. P. Morgan (finance), Andrew Carnegie (steel), and E. H. Harriman (railroads). These men, and others like them, constituted the Republican "establishment." Its power base lay in the East, in New York, in Wall Street; Washington was merely the formal seat of government where the President and such Senators as Mark Hanna and multimillionaire Nelson W. Aldrich were expected to protect the interests of the business trusts.

Roosevelt knew this, of course. He was, as he often said, "a practical man." As Governor of New York he had dealt with this invisible government by the judicious application of the principle of quid pro quo. "I am on to the crooked machines," the new President told Steffens, "and the machinists, too. Yes, even in the Congress."

"What are you going to do about them and their demands for jobs for their heelers?" Steffens asked.

"Deal with them," Roosevelt snapped. "If they'll vote for my measures I'll appoint their nominees to federal jobs. And I'm going to tell them so. They think I won't, you know. I'm going to call in a couple of machine senators and a few key congressmen and tell them I'll trade."

Steffens suggested that the President might exert more influence upon Congress if he didn't divulge his willingness to trade.

"No, no," Roosevelt insisted. "I'm going at it my own way. I want service out of the men I appoint, too. So I'm going to pass the word that I'll play the game, appoint their men for their support of my bills. But," he added, gritting his teeth and clenching his fists, "their men that I appoint have got to take my orders and obey them up to the hilt."

That was Roosevelt's way. If he couldn't get a whole loaf, he would take half a loaf—and sound as though he had gotten the whole loaf.

With Roosevelt's succession, the "velocity of administration," in the words of one newspaper, was stepped up. The new President made the White House, a name he was the first to use officially, a lively place. Politicians flowed in and out of the executive offices each morning, and reformers, writers, naturalists, prize fighters—even the first Negro, Booker T. Washington—trooped in to lunch. Work was often combined with exercise. "Under the new Administration," Secretary of War Root remarked to Senator Lodge, "horseback riding is the order of the afternoon."

Three times a week Roosevelt wrestled with Japanese instructors. "My right ankle and my left wrist and one thumb and both great toes are swollen sufficiently to more or less impair their usefulness, and I am well mottled with bruises elsewhere," he once wrote his older son, Theodore. "Still, I have made good progress, and since you left they have taught me three new throws that are perfect corkers."

In the political arena, the new President moved more cautiously. Roosevelt was a historian; he knew that Tyler and Johnson had crippled themselves by warring with the congressional leadership of their parties, that no "accidental" President ever had won a second term. "I have a very strong feeling that it is a President's duty to get on with Congress if he possibly can," he once said, "and that it is a reflection upon him if he and Congress come to a complete break."

Determined not to repeat his predecessors' mistakes, he wisely avoided risking his prestige in a showdown with the conservative congressional leadership. Instead, he compromised with them and, using the executive patronage, built his own following within the party for the convention battle of 1904.

But Roosevelt's accommodation with the conservatives did not extend to what he considered the province of executive prerogative. He believed that the President was a "steward of the people" and that "it was not only his right but his duty to do anything that the needs of the nation demanded unless such action was forbidden by the Constitution or by the laws."

Twice in 1902 Roosevelt acted upon this "stewardship" theory. The first time he threw down a challenge; the second time he picked one up.

In his annual message to Congress in 1901 Roosevelt had requested legislation which would give the government "power of supervision and regulation over all corporations doing an interstate business." Congress ignored the request, so early in 1902 Roosevelt instructed Attorney General Philander C. Knox to file an antitrust suit under the Sherman Act of 1890 to dissolve the newly formed Northern Securities Company, a giant railroad trust.

Wall Street was stunned by the President's bold action. "Not since the assassination of President McKinley has the stock market had such a sudden shock," reported the New York *Tribune*.

The Sherman Act had lain dormant for years. In 1895 the Supreme Court had ruled 8 to 1 for the sugar trust in a test case (U.S. v. E. C. Knight Co.); the decision had left the trusts free to operate without fear of prosecution. But it was the nature of Roosevelt's tactics and the size of his quarry that shook up the business community. Behind the Northern Securities Company stood the giants of American industry, J. P. Morgan, John D. Rockefeller, James J. Hill and E. H. Harriman. And no one except Knox—not even the rest of the Cabinet—had been informed in advance of the impending suit. For the first time in years the White House had not consulted Wall Street on a major business policy decision.

Morgan went to Washington to discuss the matter with Roosevelt. He was used to cooperation from the White House. "If we have done something wrong," he told the President, "send your man to my man and they can fix it up."

"That can't be done," Roosevelt replied dryly. He was annoyed that Morgan should treat the President of the United States like a rival businessman.

And Knox, who was present, added, "We don't want to fix it up, we want to stop it."

Morgan reportedly wrote Roosevelt a blistering let-

ter when he returned to his hotel but was persuaded
not to send it.

A year later Roosevelt won the Northern Securities
suit, and in 1904 the Supreme Court, reversing its 1895
opinion, upheld the verdict, 5 to 4. It was an impressive victory. The President gained prestige and public
acclaim, and he proved that he was both willing and
able to use the powers of the presidency. "Morgan
no longer rules the earth," wrote one observer.

Roosevelt's Northern Securities victory revived the
moribund Sherman Act. McKinley had not once invoked the antitrust law; Roosevelt, in the next seven
years, initiated 44 suits, moving against such companies as Standard Oil, American Tobacco and DuPont.
"The Northern Securities suit is one of the great
achievements of my administration," Roosevelt later
wrote. "I look back upon it with great pride, for
through it we emphasized in signal fashion, as in no
other way could be emphasized, the fact that the most
powerful men in this country were held to accounta-
bility before the law." For the phrase "before the
law" one can safely substitute "before the President."

Shortly after filing the Northern Securities suit,
Roosevelt had a challenge thrust upon him by the coal
mining industry. In May the anthracite miners went
on strike, demanding a 10 to 20 percent pay increase,
an eight-hour day and recognition of the United Mine
Workers Union. The mine operators refused even to
negotiate with the union. Instead they closed down
the mines, confident that starvation at home and a fuel
shortage in the large eastern cities would force the

miners back to work. But the union refused to crack, and the strike dragged on through the summer and into the fall.

The mine operators remained adamant. They had reluctantly given the miners a 10 percent wage increase in 1900 when Mark Hanna, fearful of the effect of a prolonged strike in an election year, had persuaded them that a concession was worth four more years of McKinleyism. And then they had gotten that upstart Roosevelt. Now they refused all offers of mediation, the President's included, and declared there would be no compromise. Public opinion hardened against the operator's obstinate stand.

Meanwhile, Roosevelt narrowly escaped death in Pittsfield, Massachusetts, when a speeding trolley smashed into his carriage. A secret service guard riding on the box with the driver was killed; Roosevelt was hurled 40 feet from his seat. But for the matter of a split second, Secretary of State John Hay would have become the 27th President of the United States.

As October began and temperatures dropped, the coal situation became critical. Coal reserves had dwindled to zero; homeowners, hospitals and schools were faced with a bleak, cold winter. Municipal officials in Boston and New York predicted widespread rioting if the impasse continued.

On October 3rd, Roosevelt called union and management officials to a White House conference. He explained that the urgency of the situation had made his action necessary. Union officials repeated their offer to negotiate with the operators or to accept the findings of an arbitration commission appointed by the President. The operators, however, balked at all proposals. They refused even to talk to the union officials and demanded that the President prosecute the union under the antitrust laws. The conference ended in failure.

Roosevelt was incensed by the "arrogant stupidity" and "gross blindness" of the operators. "They fail absolutely to understand that they have any duty toward the public," he told a friend. Convinced that the mine operators were acting unreasonably, the President prepared to seize the mines and operate them with federal troops.

This was nowhere sanctioned in the Constitution; Roosevelt knew that. He was setting this "evil" precedent, he explained, "rather than expose our people to the suffering and chaos which would otherwise come." The mine operators, faced with this "terrible specter of state socialism," reluctantly agreed to arbitration. A commission was appointed, and on October 21st the mines were reopened. Five months later, the commission awarded the miners a 10 percent wage increase and a nine-hour day but withheld recognition of the union. They also recommended a 10 percent increase in the price of coal, a suggestion the operators quickly followed.

The settlement was Roosevelt's first great presidential triumph. It made the government, for the first time, a powerful "third force" in labor-management relations and won him widespread popular support—which support, in turn, increased his moral and political influence.

Roosevelt used this influence to the fullest. In 1903 he, in his own words, "took the Canal Zone" in Panama when Colombia would not meet his terms. (Ten years later the United States offered Colombia apologies and compensation of $25 million for the action.) In 1905 he sent marines to Santo Domingo to clean up corruption in that island's government and forestall European intervention in its affairs. "Chronic wrongdoing, or an impotence which results in a general loosening of the ties of civilized society," Roosevelt explained, "may in America, as elsewhere, ultimately require intervention by some civilized nation, and in the Western Hemisphere the adherence of the United States to the Monroe Doctrine may force the United States . . . to the exercise of an international police power." This policy became known as the "Roosevelt Corollary" to the Monroe Doctrine.

The President did not consult with Congress on these ventures. In his opinion, a legislative body was "not fitted for the shaping of foreign policy." When he sent the fleet around the world to "show the flag" in 1907, many Congressmen opposed taking the fleet from Atlantic waters. One Senator reminded the President that Congress could withhold the funds for the voyage. Roosevelt replied that he had enough money to get the fleet to the Pacific "and that if Congress did not choose to appropriate enough money to get the fleet back, why, it could stay in the Pacific." He got the money.

But it was only after 1904 that Roosevelt felt he had a free hand. Until then his ambition to succeed himself tempered his actions. Roosevelt, notes one historian, spent his first term running for a second term. His only serious rival for the Republican nomination was Hanna, Wall Street's man. The President was busy undermining Hanna's support when in February, 1904, Hanna died, leaving Roosevelt a clear path to the nomination. In June the convention dutifully nominated Roosevelt in an atmosphere "of feigned enthusiasm punctuated by indifference." He was the first "Vice-President of destiny" to win the presidential nomination on his own.

The convention chose as Roosevelt's running mate Senator Charles Warren Fairbanks, a wealthy Indianan who was so conservative he was known as "Icebanks." The President disliked Fairbanks; indeed, the two men were totally incompatible. In 1896 Roosevelt had said, "It is an unhealthy thing to have the Vice-President and President represented by principles so far apart that the succession of one to the place of the other means a change as radical as any party overturn." But in 1904 he accepted just that situation. It was another instance of half a loaf is better than none, and in this case the half a loaf was Wall Street campaign money.

In July the Democrats nominated for President a New York conservative, Judge Alton B. Parker, and chose as his running mate an eighty-one-year-old millionaire, Henry G. Davis. They were swamped. Promising a "square deal" for everyone, Roosevelt won all but the 13 southern states and rolled up a record margin of nearly 2,600,000 votes over Parker. A few days later the President, meeting a leading conservative Senator, greeted him with, "You are shaking hands with His Excellency, not His Accidency."

Roosevelt in his second term became the reformer he always had claimed to be. In 1906 he pushed through the Senate ("the graveyard of reform legislation") the Pure Food and Drug Act and the Meat Inspection Act to correct long-standing abuses in these areas. He also got from a reluctant Senate a bill to regulate the railroads, the Hepburn Act. Although it was necessarily a compromise measure, historian George E. Mowry calls the act "a landmark in the evolution of federal control of private industry." Meanwhile, despite the constant harassment of the conservatives in Congress, Roosevelt stepped up antitrust action and enlarged upon his conservation policies.

By 1907 he saw himself as "trying to keep the left center together." A year later he described himself as a "radical" and declared that the workingman should be guaranteed a larger share of the wealth that is produced. At the same time he denounced the "malefactors of great wealth" and sent to Congress requests for an income and inheritance tax, regulation of stock market gambling, stricter fixing of railroad rates, national incorporation and regulation of interstate business, compulsory investigations of large labor disputes and extension of the eight-hour day and workingmen's compensation—all measures that were far ahead of their time.

But Congress paid no heed to these requests. By 1908 Roosevelt had abandoned his accommodation tactics, and the conservatives had written him off as too radical. The result was, in Roosevelt's words, a "period of stagnation" which "continued to rage with uninterrupted violence."

Roosevelt had weakened his own position by announcing, in 1904, that he would not seek reelection in 1908. It was one of his few political mistakes. The President, says Richard E. Neustadt in his excellent book, *Presidential Power,* should "induce as much uncertainty as possible about the consequences of ignoring what he wants." Roosevelt's early disclosure of his intentions left his opponents free to cross him without risk. He himself had second thoughts about his decision when the time came to act on it. "I should like to have stayed on in the presidency," he told a friend, "and I make no pretense that I am glad to be relieved of my official duties."

The nomination was his for the taking. But he considered his word binding, and he believed in the two-term tradition, so he named as his heir a stodgy patrician, William Howard Taft, whom he thought would continue his reform policies.

William Jennings Bryan, for the third time, was the Democratic nominee. Taft easily defeated him in the election and Roosevelt, shortly after his successor's inauguration, sailed for Africa to hunt big game. ("Health to the lions," J. P. Morgan is said to have remarked.) "I have finished my career in public life," Roosevelt announced. "I have enjoyed it to the full." And to his friend Frederick Remington, the painter, he wrote, "I have had about as good a run for my money as any human being possibly could have; and whatever happens to me now I am ahead of the game."

Taft, however, failed to live up to Roosevelt's expectations. A conservative at heart, he was—unlike Roosevelt—out of touch with the times, and he made at best an indifferent record as President. "Compared to the Presidents who preceded and followed him, Taft was lazy," says George E. Mowry, adding, ". . . he was always reluctant to leave a game to get back to work." By 1911 Roosevelt was writing to a friend, "Taft is utterly hopeless." In 1912 he announced, "My hat is in the ring," and attempted to unseat his heir.

Unable to prevent Taft's nomination by the Republicans, Roosevelt broke with the party and ran on a Progressive ("Bull Moose") ticket. Meanwhile, the Democrats, on the 46th ballot, nominated Woodrow Wilson, who just two years previously had been president of Princeton University.

At the height of the election campaign, Roosevelt was shot in the chest by a half-crazed fanatic in Milwaukee. He had been on his way to give a speech, and he insisted on keeping his appointment. "I shall make this speech, or die," he told the doctors examining him. From the podium he asked his audience for quiet and to excuse him from making a long speech. "I'll do the best I can," he said, "but you see there is a bullet in my body."

He removed a folded copy of his speech from the breast pocket of his coat. There was a bullet hole completely through it—and through his metal spectacle case. Roosevelt, always the showman, held up the perforated paper. "It takes more than that," he told the audience, "to kill a Bull Moose!"

The spectacle case and folded speech had deflected the bullet upward into Roosevelt's chest muscles. Had they not done so, said an attending physician, "Roosevelt would not have lived sixty seconds." The former President shrugged off the incident as "a trade risk, which every prominent public man ought to accept as a matter of course."

With the Republican vote divided, Wilson easily won the election. Roosevelt came in second. He had expected as much. There was, he had said in July, "some small chance of victory, but not enough for us to take into account."

After his defeat, Roosevelt became an elder statesman. In 1914, the great European war aroused his martial spirit—which was never more than dormant. But Wilson first delayed America's entry into the struggle, then denied Roosevelt's request to lead a combat division. Roosevelt never forgave him for that. He had to be content to send his four sons (he also had two daughters) to war. Each of them served gallantly, and the youngest, Quentin, was killed in action. "It is a very sad thing," he wrote, "to see the young die when the old who are doing nothing, as I am doing nothing, are left alive."

Six months later, on January 6, 1919, Roosevelt himself died peacefully in his sleep after a short illness. His life ended as his supporters were boosting him for the Republican presidential nomination in 1920. He had been receptive to the idea, for he liked to be in the center of the action, calling the shots. As a young man he had resolved to belong "to the governing class and not to the governed." He had achieved that aim, although Lincoln Steffens insisted that Roosevelt "governed with the consent of the governors."

His record was like an inverted iceberg. The bulk of it, above the surface, was encrusted with rhetoric and rationalization. Below the surface, the mass was smaller but it was solid with achievement. One of those achievements was making the presidency an instrument of public policy at a time when the public was at the mercy of a crass business oligarchy. As historian Mowry notes, Roosevelt "proposed practically every reform that was to be made during the Taft and Wilson administrations, and even a few, it might be added, that were to lie inanimate until the New Deal days."

He did not "speak softly and carry a big stick." More often, he spoke loudly and held out a carrot. Nor was he a "trust buster." He believed in regulation, not dissolution, of corporations. "We do not wish to destroy corporations," he said, "but we do wish to make them subserve the public good."

Roosevelt knew instinctively, as Lincoln did and Andrew Johnson did not, how to wield presidential power. Summing up his seven years in the presidency, he told his good friend, the English historian Sir George Otto Trevelyan, "While President, I have *been* President, emphatically; I have used every ounce of power there was in the office . . . I have felt not merely that my action was right in itself but that in showing the strength of, or in giving strength to, the executive, I was establishing a precedent of value."

That, perhaps, is his most enduring legacy.

My first thought was that I could swing it.

—CALVIN COOLIDGE's reaction to his succession to the presidency

6 Calvin Coolidge: 1923

The death of Theodore Roosevelt in 1919 signaled the beginning of musical chairs for the Republican presidential nomination of 1920. At stake, all the players were sure, was the presidential chair; for Americans, tired of World War I and its bitter aftermath, were ready for a change, and the Republicans, the "out" party, were expected to win easily in November.

The party faithful convened in Chicago in June to choose a standard-bearer. Of the many candidates who came prepared to serve, four stood out. General Leonard Wood, who had fought beside Roosevelt in Cuba, was billed as his logical heir. His chief rival was Governor Frank O. Lowden of Illinois, a man of substantial means and modest ends. Trailing the leaders was the radical progressive, Senator Hiram Johnson of California, who had been Roosevelt's Vice-President in his unsuccessful 1912 Bull Moose campaign. And waiting patiently in the wings was the handsome, affable Senator Warren G. Harding of Ohio, a "regular he-man" and "great poker player."

The first ballot was taken in the hot, crowded auditorium of the Coliseum, a building that once had served as a prison. General Wood led with 287 votes, Governor Lowden had 211, Senator Johnson had 113, Senator Harding had 65, and 14 other aspirants shared the rest. Four hundred and ninety-three votes were needed for the nomination, and the candidates now began to trade for them.

But after four ballots the situation remained substantially the same. Wood and Lowden held fast, each hoping to crack the other. Johnson stood pat, banking on becoming a compromise choice. He had no chance; the party conservatives had too much power to let the radical Johnson go anywhere but through the eye of a needle. His support, however, might tip the balance of power elsewhere, so his rivals offered him the vice-presidency in return for his endorsement. Johnson declined, preferring to head the ticket or return to the Senate.

"There isn't a thing under the sun that I haven't been offered during the last week," he said. "It is singular that the very gentlemen who have been equally insistent on my taking the vice-presidency had been equally insistent that I was utterly unfit to be President, although there is only a heartbeat between the two."

To Harding's offer of second place on the ticket Johnson was more explicit. "We are living in a day of strange events," he told Harding's emissary, "but none

so strange as that I should be considered second to Senator Harding."

Meanwhile, Harding, vigorously fanning himself in a muggy hotel room, fretted about his hotel bill and vowed to quit politics if he were not nominated.

He need not have worried. With the Wood and Lowden forces deadlocked, control of the convention passed to a junta of conservative Senators who were eager to restore to the Senate the power that they felt had been usurped by such strong Presidents as Roosevelt and Wilson. The Senators were wary of Wood, uncertain of Lowden and unalterably opposed to Johnson. They wanted a candidate who, "when elected, would sign whatever bills the Senate sent him and not send bills to the Senate to pass." Warren G. Harding, they decided in a "smoke-filled" hotel room, was their man. He could be expected to look like a President without acting like one.

On the 10th ballot Harding was nominated. The next order of business for the tired, sweaty delegates was to fill the second spot on the ticket. The junta's choice was another Senator, Irvine H. Lenroot of Wisconsin, whose faint tincture of "progressivism" was meant to mollify the liberal faction of the party. Some of the delegates, resigned to Lenroot's nomination, began shuffling out of the hall. But others revolted. As Lenroot was being praised in a nominating speech, cries of "Coolidge!" rose from the floor. A moment later an obscure delegate was shouting: ". . . and on behalf of the Oregon delegation I name for the exalted office of Vice-President, Governor Calvin Coolidge of

Massachusetts!" Amid the turmoil the only word that came through clearly was "Coolidge!" It was enough. The delegates, remembering the leatherbound, personally embossed book *Have Faith in Massachusetts* that Coolidge's emissaries had distributed among them, asserted their independence by nominating the Massachusetts Governor over Lenroot on the first ballot, 674 to 146.

Coolidge was in Boston with his wife when the news came over the telephone. "You aren't going to take it, are you?" Mrs. Coolidge asked her husband politely.

"Well—I suppose I'll have to," he replied.

And so Calvin Coolidge, who only a dozen years before had been, in the words of his biographer, "a second rate lawyer in a fourth class town," sidled up to the second highest office in the land.

Luck is the residue of sweat. It was typical of Coolidge that when a break came, as in the delegates' revolt against the Senate junta, he was prepared to turn it to his advantage. Coolidge always did his political homework. "I meant to be ready," he once said, "to take advantage of opportunities." If Chester Arthur could be said to have drifted into success, Calvin Coolidge could be said to have sailed into it—always with a firm hand on the tiller.

He was born in 1872 in Plymouth, Vermont, a tiny village of rocky soil, Puritan ethics and Republican politics. The combination most often produces a parsimony of mind and spirit, and Coolidge was no exception. It was said of him that he pronounced "cow" in three syllables, but that he never pronounced it at all unless there was a compelling reason.

Coolidge was named after his father, John (the name was dropped in childhood), but he favored his mother. She was a delicate, fair-skinned woman who liked to "gaze at the purple sunsets and watch the evening stars." Coolidge was only thirteen when she died. "Life was never to me the same again," he wrote later. When he grew up, he carried her picture everywhere.

The Coolidges were one of the leading families of Plymouth. John Coolidge ran a small farm and a country store. At one time or another he held all the local offices—selectman, road commissioner, constable, justice of the peace, tax collector—and he served four terms in the Vermont legislature. So, young Coolidge learned politics early.

From the beginning, however, he was shy with people. When anyone came and sat in the kitchen with his parents, he said, "the hardest thing in the world for me was to have to go through that door and greet the visitors. . . . Every time I meet a stranger," he added, "I have to stand by that old kitchen door a minute."

As a student his habits overshadowed his scholarship. His grade school teacher described him as "methodical, faithful, honest and punctual, never tardy, never much ahead of time." In high school he was remembered for a prank he didn't commit. Some boys pulled a stove down the stairs of the dormitory. Coolidge was asleep, but of course the clatter woke him. Later the teacher wanted to know why he didn't do something, give an alarm. "It wa'n't my stove," Coolidge replied casually.

His record at Amherst College was similiar—gray, prudent. He was an outsider, an invisible man. Though he coveted fraternity membership, he was not pledged until his senior year—and then only by a new fraternity seeking to build up a membership. Thin, pale, withdrawn, he lingered around the edges of events. A dinner companion once asked him if he had participated in sports in college. "Yes," he answered, munching a nut, "I held stakes."

He did, however, run a race once, in a high hat. It was the annual ritual of the junior class in which the loser had to make a speech. Coolidge came in last and made a funny speech, which ended prophetically. "Remember, boys," he said, his blue eyes twinkling, "there are firsts that shall be last and the last first."

Meanwhile, the Puritan traditions that he had been weaned on—prudence, piety and property—were invested with the dignity of philosophy at Amherst. Describing his conclusions at this time, Coolidge later wrote, in part, ". . . people are entitled to the rewards of their industry. What they earn is theirs, no matter how small or how great. But the possession of property carries the obligation to use it in a larger service." Coolidge revered money and equated it with respectability. This was at once the source of his strength, because most Americans share this attitude, and the core of his weakness, because it is an attitude that narrows rather than broadens one's horizons.

In 1895 he was graduated from Amherst. He had

decided to study law, and a friend asked him where he would serve his apprenticeship. "Northampton," replied Coolidge, "is the nearest courthouse," and there he went.

Northhampton was a small manufacturing town in which the reward of industry was property and property's obligations were discharged in philanthropy. Coolidge was taken on as a clerk in a local law office. He read law during the day and Shakespeare, Milton and Kipling at night, and after only 20 months passed the state bar examination and went into practice for himself. At the same time he settled into Republican precinct politics.

The neighborhood precinct lies at the base of the American political pyramid. From the precinct, power flows upward. District leaders choose candidates for local and county offices, the state legislature and the House of Representatives; district delegates to the state convention vote (or, if they have the power, *dictate*) their choice of candidates for the U. S. Senate, the governorship and other state offices; and every four years they join the state delegations that convene to nominate a President and Vice-President.

This is the party machine. Powered by precinct workers and greased by money and favors, it has a life of its own. A man can win without it, or even against it, but he cannot destroy it. Herbert Croly, the famous editor and founder of *The New Republic,* once said that the two American political parties are indestructible because they are low-grade organisms without a brain or a heart and even if they were cut in pieces the bleeding fragments somehow would wiggle on and survive.

With his typical foresight, Coolidge had taken lodgings in Northhampton's "silk stocking" district, Ward Two. Here lived the politicians who ran the party and the businessmen who controlled the politicians. Coolidge, starting at the bottom of the machine as a precinct worker, slowly floated to the top. In 1896 he stumped for McKinley. Thereafter he ran errands, attended party meetings and functions, listened much and said little. He did what was asked of him and asked nothing for himself. Before he was thirty years old he was the district leader of Ward Two and the vice-president of a local savings bank. By 1904 he was the top Republican in Northhampton and a rising power in state politics. In his spare time, he practiced law.

He also ran for office. In 1899 he won a seat on Northhampton's City Council (where his first official act was to offer a resolution of respect for a dead Democratic councilman). The following year he was elected city solicitor, a job he sought because he thought it would make him "a better lawyer." In 1903 he was appointed clerk of the court for Hampshire County. The job paid $2,300, much more than Coolidge ever had earned, but he declined to stand for election. Money was not important to him except to save, and his legendary frugality was more a way of life than an economic necessity; he was as frugal with his emotions as with his money.

Later temptations were greater. While a state

senator he was offered the vice-presidency of a successful insurance company and promised the presidency
upon the death of the president, who was incurably ill.
The salary would have started at $25,000 and risen to
$50,000. "No," Coolidge replied to the offer, the
initial salary of which was more than ten times what
he was making, "that doesn't lie along my line of
influence."

In 1905 Coolidge married Grace Goodhue, a lovely,
vivacious young woman who taught at the local school
for the deaf and dumb. "We thought we were made
for each other," Coolidge wrote 25 years later. "For
almost a quarter of a century she has borne with my
infirmities and I have rejoiced in her graces."

Coolidge's description of his marriage was as true
as it was chivalrous. Although he was cool in public,
privately Coolidge was irascible and volatile. Theodore Roosevelt in his worst rage was placid compared
to Coolidge, according to the White House usher who
served them both. At the same time, Coolidge was a
remarkably uncommunicative person. He often sat
through meals without saying a word, and at social
affairs he left an awkward silence in his wake. One
man remembers that in five hours at his side Coolidge
spoke to him just once. On another occasion a society
matron cornered Coolidge and told him she had bet
a friend that she could make him say more than two
words. "You lose," Coolidge snapped and turned
away.

It was left to Grace Coolidge to fill the gaps left
by her husband's gaucheness, bear him two sons and

run a household on a shoestring budget. She didn't seem to mind it. Coolidge, for his part, worked at politics by day and at night read in bed "to improve his mind" and translated Dante's *Inferno* from the Italian.

Three months after his marriage Coolidge suffered his only defeat at the polls while running for the local school board. But the next year he was elected to the Massachusetts House of Representatives. He went the 100 miles to Boston with two suits and a note of introduction from an ex-legislator to the speaker-elect of the House. The note said of Coolidge: "Like a singed cat, he is better than he looks."

After two undistinguished terms in the Massachusetts House, Coolidge won two terms as Mayor of Northampton. Then, in 1912, he returned to Boston. this time as state senator.

For the record he voted for a state income tax, the right to picket, direct nomination of U.S. Senators and woman suffrage. But, in vital committee assignments, he remained a regular, working diligently, preaching economy and defending "the rights of private property owners."

His regularity attracted powerful backers. Senator Murray Crane, the ruler of western Massachusetts (Senator Henry Cabot Lodge, Cranes archrival, ruled the eastern enclave), threw his influence and machine behind Coolidge. Guy Currier, a cultivated collector of politicians, provided him with connections and political expertise. Frank Stearns, a wealthy merchant, lavished upon him adoration and dedication and spent whatever sums were required to further Coolidge's career.

In rapid succession Coolidge became president of the senate, Lieutenant Governor and, in 1918, Governor. At the time, he said later, he would have been content to close his political career as Governor; he thought he had gone as far as he could go. But, in 1919, he suddenly was thrust into national prominence.

The stage had been set by the Great War and the Russian Revolution. War had accustomed Americans to regimentation, crusading and violence; and the revolution had kept alive the fervor of these drives. Some Americans saw the revolution as a fresh wind that would sweep away a brutalizing economic system; others saw it as a threat to freedom and stability.

Social discontent and labor agitation surfaced in the nation's cities. The solid middle class—white-collar workers, small businessmen, homeowners, war veterans—reacted with confusion, hysteria and super-patriotism. They were anxious. Attorney General A. Mitchell Palmer saw the strikes and demonstrations as part of a vast Bolshevik conspiracy. "Like a prairie-fire, the blaze of revolution was . . . eating its way into the homes of the American workman," Palmer insisted. Later his agents raided "radical centers" throughout the country, capturing more than 6,000 "revolutionaries"—and three revolvers.

In this setting, the Boston police went out on strike when their union leaders were punished for affiliating with the American Federation of Labor. Neither Governor Coolidge, a Republican, nor the Mayor of

Boston, a Democrat, wanted to offend labor by calling out the militia. Looting and rioting followed in which two people were killed. Now Coolidge's associates advised him to use his authority to take command of the situation from the Mayor. He did, and Samuel Gompers, the head of the A. F. of L., singled out the Governor for rebuke. Coolidge made the most of this opening and wired back: "The right of the police of Boston to affiliate has always been questioned, never granted, is now prohibited. . . . There is no right to strike against the public safety by anybody, anywhere, anytime." Overnight, he became a national hero.

The Mayor had taken the action, but Coolidge, with his succinct statement, reaped the rewards. A year later his notoriety vaulted him into the vice-presidency.

Coolidge found it "especially agreeable" to be associated with Senator Harding. Harding announced that "the country needs the counsel and the becoming [*sic*] participation in government of such men as Calvin Coolidge." Little more was said—or needed. That November, Harding and Coolidge, the Laurel and Hardy of American politics, were swept into office by almost a two-to-one margin over Democrats James M. Cox and Franklin D. Roosevelt. The age of "normalcy" had begun.

Settling into the obscurity of his office, Coolidge presided over the Senate—one of the ablest parliamentarians ever to do so—and sat through endless ceremonial dinners. One of his hostesses, noting his customary silence, remarked how hard it must be to attend so many official dinners. "Have to eat some-where," Coolidge replied.

Harding invited the Vice-President to attend Cabinet meetings regularly, to bring him "into the councils." Coolidge readily accepted the invitation. The Vice-President, he agreed, "should be in the Cabinet because he might become President and ought to be informed on the policies of the Administration." It was one of his more constructive thoughts and, as it turned out, an unwitting prophecy.

With Harding's real inner circle, however, Coolidge had scant contact. These were Harding's old cronies—Ohio clubhouse hacks, lobbyists and fixers such as his chief booster, Harry M. Daugherty—whom he had appointed to high office. While the President played poker with them in the White House, they played their own games with federal contracts and the public treasury. Historian Frederick Lewis Allen estimates that "the Harding Administration was responsible in its two short years and five months for more concentrated robbery and rascality than any other in the whole history of the federal government."

Through it all, Vice-President Coolidge kept a tight lip and stern demeanor. His sensitive nose must have detected the odor of scandal, but none of it contaminated him. He was, as his biographer William Allen White dubbed him, "a Puritan in Babylon."

By the summer of 1923, however, the smell of corruption no longer could be avoided. Congressmen were probing the Interior Department's handling of certain oil leases; the director of the Veterans Bureau, a Harding appointee, had resigned after stealing $250,000, and another Bureau official had committed suicide; and in the Justice Department, one of the President's inner circle had burned his papers and shot himself when threatened by Harding with arrest. "My God, this is a hell of a job," the President told a reporter. "I have no trouble with my enemies. . . . But my damned friends . . . keep me walking the floor nights."

Harding decided to take a trip to Alaska. On the voyage there, he compulsively played bridge and nervously alluded to "a great scandal" in his administration. Returning from Alaska, he was stricken in Seattle with what was diagnosed as ptomaine poisoning from eating crab meat—though no crab meat was on the official menu. He was moved to San Francisco, where he contracted pneumonia. After a few days his doctors declared him out of danger; then, in the evening of August 2nd, he suffered a sudden "stroke of apoplexy" and died. "No one can hurt you now, Warren," said Mrs. Harding.

There has been speculation that Harding took poison or was given it by his wife. She was alone with him when he suffered his fatal "stroke," and no autopsy ever was performed to confirm the cause of death. One theory is that Harding could neither face disgrace nor expose his betrayers and so chose suicide. Another is that Mrs. Harding, jealous of her husband's mistresses (he had at least two) and of his reputation, poisoned him to spite the former and preserve the latter.

Either theory is plausible; each fits the characters of the principal actors and the vulnerability to violence of the presidency, a vulnerability that has been demonstrated at least four times in less than a hundred years. Of course, Harding very well may have died from some kind of stroke; he was overweight and overwrought. But without an autopsy, no one can be certain. The only certainty is that, whatever killed him, Harding had lost the will to live.

Calvin Coolidge, asleep in his father's cottage in Plymouth, was awakened a few hours later by a persistent pounding at the door. "What's wanted?" he heard his father call down into the darkness. "President Harding is dead," a breathless messenger cried, "and I have a telegram for the Vice-President!" Coolidge had become the 30th President of the United States.

"My first thought was that I could swing it," he said later.

He took the oath of office from his father (who was a notary public), then dictated a statement that he would continue Harding's policies, retain the Cabinet members and trust the direction of the nation's destinies to God. A few friends were present. Coolidge stood among them, in the glow of a kerosene lamp, straight-backed, controlled, colorless, looking more like a mortician than President.

But he was President, and the challenges now were his to face. The first one was not long in coming.

A Senate committee had investigated those questionable oil leases. What they found was that Harding's

Secretary of the Interior, Albert B. Fall, had persuaded the late President to transfer control of the naval oil reserves at Teapot Dome in Wyoming and Elk Hills in California from the Navy Department to his own jurisdiction. Fall then had leased Teapot Dome to Harry F. Sinclair's Mammoth Oil Company and Elk Hills to Edward L. Doheny's Pan-American Petroleum Company. Coincidentally, Sinclair had given Fall $223,000 in government bonds, $85,000 in cash and a herd of cattle for his ranch; and Doheny had "lent" Fall $100,000.

The public's veneration of the dead President quickly turned to indignation, and this increased as further scandals were revealed. Cries for Daugherty's resignation as Attorney General were raised in public and in Congress. Coolidge, however, did nothing. He regarded the Teapot Dome investigation as a Democratic plot; and he declined to remove Daugherty, the one man for whom, as he said, "President Harding would more surely demand his day in court, would more surely *not* dismiss because of popular clamor."

But, as the investigation wore on and it became clear that it was not a partisan plot, and as the 1924 elections drew near, President Coolidge acted. He appointed his own counsel (a Democrat and a Republican) to prosecute the oil cases and, three days later, removed Daugherty—ostensibly for refusing to give the Senate investigating committee certain official papers. "Let the guilty be punished," Coolidge told reporters.

The case dragged in and out of the courts for years.

Ultimately the oil leases were voided and Fall went to jail for accepting a bribe. Doheny and Sinclair were acquitted of conspiracy to defraud the government, but Sinclair went to jail for contempt of Congress and for tampering with a jury. Daugherty was tried for complicity in various scandals but managed to win a hung jury.

Meanwhile, Coolidge faced his second challenge: winning the 1924 Republican nomination for President on his own. Theodore Roosevelt had done it in 1904 by speaking loudly and quietly garnering convention delegates; Coolidge did it in 1924 by remaining silent and quietly garnering convention delegates. At the convention, he won all but 44 of the 1,109 delegates' votes.

Coolidge wanted Senator William E. Borah as Vice-President, but Borah didn't seem to want the job. The still-powerful Senate junta, which didn't want Borah, then secured the nomination of Chicago banker and party regular Charles G. Dawes, who had made a name on the German reparations commission. Nobody, except Dawes, was enthusiastic about the choice. Once again, the vice-presidency had been filled as an afterthought.

The election itself might have been expected to be close since Coolidge had to contend with the shadow of the Harding scandals. But the Democrats insured a Republican victory by splitting into Alfred E. Smith and William G. McAdoo factions. The convention delegates remained hopelessly divided for 102 ballots; on the 103rd roll call, John W. Davis, a corporation lawyer, was nominated as a compromise candidate. Charles Bryan, William Jennings Bryan's younger brother, was chosen as Davis' running mate.

Senator Robert LaFollette entered the race as a Progressive and chose as his running mate Senator Burton K. Wheeler of Montana, who was assisting in the Teapot Dome investigation. Dawes, who did the Republican campaigning, pictured the voter's alternatives as "whether you stand on the rock of common sense with Calvin Coolidge or on the sinking sands of socialism," meaning LaFollette's program. Davis, in exasperation, attacked the Republican campaign as a "vast, pervading and mysterious silence, broken only by Dawes warning the American people that under every bedstead lurks a Bolshevik ready to destroy them."

Coolidge was an easy winner. He polled almost twice as many votes as Davis, and his margin in the electoral college was 382 to 136. LaFollette polled almost 5 million votes but won only his own state, Wisconsin.

Harding normalcy gave way to Coolidge prosperity. "The business of America is business," Coolidge had said, and Americans now settled down to making money. Business itself became a religion. Businessmen extolled the "spiritual principles in advertising," called Moses "one of the greatest salesmen and real estate promoters that ever lived" and portrayed Jesus as a great executive who "picked up twelve men from the bottom ranks of business and forged them into an organization that conquered the world."

In the stock market, the temple of the faithful, the money changers and gamblers were busy. Stocks soared upward but on speculative wings so fragile that within a few years they would disintegrate and bring the entire business structure crashing down.

The machinations of the market was one of the problems Coolidge never faced. He didn't understand it. Toward the end of his presidency, he sensed that the market was oversold, but he didn't know what to do about it so he did nothing. He had entrusted fiscal affairs to his Secretary of the Treasury, Andrew W. Mellon, a multimillionaire whose policy was to reduce the taxes of the rich. Coolidge, "persuaded of the divine character of wealth," as historian Arthur M. Schlesinger, Jr., notes, went along with multi-millionaire Mellon. If a million could do no wrong, he reasoned, 100 million guaranteed a positive genius for doing right.

While Americans frenetically pursued money and pleasure, Coolidge remained the "Puritan in Babylon." From the beginning of his presidency Coolidge served notice that the frivolity encouraged by his predecessor would not be tolerated. "I want things as they used to be—before!" he told the head usher of the executive mansion. And a visitor there, shortly after the succession, found the changed atmosphere "as different as a New England front parlor is from a back room in a speak-easy."

Coolidge set a leisurely pace. He breakfasted promptly at eight, usually on pancakes with Vermont maple syrup. From nine to twelve-thirty he worked, then broke for lunch. In the afternoon he worked another hour or two, then quit for the day. It was a light schedule. "No other President in my time," said the White House's head usher, "ever slept so much."

That was Coolidge's way—to do nothing, if possible. His favorite maxim was never to do anything that someone else could do for you. A Senator once burst into Coolidge's office and demanded that something be done about a pressing problem. The President, his feet on his desk, replied, "Don't you know that four-fifths of all our troubles in this life would disappear if we would only sit down and keep still?"

Fortunately, no crisis arose to test this theory, which worked well for Coolidge. His major accomplishment, in fact, was an action in Mexico that he didn't take.

The Mexican Revolution of 1910 had resulted in the expropriation of substantial American oil and mineral investments in Mexico, and since that time, pressure on Washington to suppress the revolution had been strong. World War I had prevented intervention in 1916, but by the mid-Twenties America's hands were free and large masses of trained veterans were available for action. Agitation for intervention mounted, but Coolidge refused to panic. Instead he appointed Dwight W. Morrow, a college friend and prominent Wall Street broker, Ambassador to Mexico and delegated him to negotiate a settlement. Morrow was successful, and the pressure for intervention subsided and eventually was replaced by the present amity between the two countries.

Political analyst Walter Lippmann sees this decision

as "a monument to the wisdom and restraint of a great power which resisted all manner of provocation and temptation. The settlement which Coolidge and Morrow made with the Mexican Revolution," Mr. Lippmann adds, "has paid handsome dividends."

It was the last challenge Coolidge met. In 1927 he issued his famous statement, "I do not choose to run for President in 1928." Whether or not he meant to be taken seriously, no one is sure. A second term on his own would have given Coolidge ten years in the White House, "longer than any other man has had it— too long!" he told a friend. But, when a newspaperman asked Coolidge whether he would be glad to retire from public life, the President replied, after a pause, "No." Probably he wished to provoke a draft, but no draft was forthcoming, one of the few instances when Coolidge's policy of doing nothing failed him. In the end the nomination was won by Secretary of Commerce Herbert Hoover, of whom Coolidge remarked, "That man has given me unsolicited advice for six years, all of it bad!"

Hoover, of course, reaped what Coolidge's financial policies (or lack of them) had helped sow—depression. Perhaps the shrewd Vermonter sensed what was coming. "I think I know myself very well," he told one Senator. "I fitted into the situation that existed right after the war, but I might not fit into the next one. . . . From this time on, there must be something constructive applied to the affairs of government, and it will not be sufficient to say, 'Let business take care of itself.' "

With that sentiment, Calvin Coolidge passed into private life. He wrote his *Autobiography* and bought a huge house in Northampton, where he sat and counted the cars that passed by and watched the country slide into depression. He was not well. Although he was not yet sixty-one, he told a friend in January, 1933, "I am all burned out." Five days later he died of a stroke while shaving.

He left on the record a few pungent epigrams, some gathering myths and little else. His presidency was one of consistency rather than achievement. He had as much training for the office as any President, but what he learned was the form of administration, not the content of leadership.

There is, of course, the question of whether or not presidential leadership can be learned. This was answered by Harry S. Truman in 1945.

Boys, if you ever pray, pray for me now. . . .
I've got the most terribly responsible job a man
ever had.

—HARRY S. TRUMAN to re-
porters after his succession

7 Harry S. Truman: 1945

Harry S. Truman was the third Vice-President to
serve under Franklin D. Roosevelt. The first one,
John Nance Garner, had fallen out with Roosevelt,
and the second one, Henry A. Wallace, had proven
to be a political liability. So, when a weary Roosevelt
prepared to run for a fourth term, the party bosses
persuaded him to dump Wallace for a "safer" running
mate. It was one of the few instances in presidential
politics when a Vice-President was picked for his potential as a successor. Political analyst Arthur Krock
called the 1944 vice-presidential nomination "of
greater importance than at any time in American
history."

Roosevelt encouraged several eager candidates, including Wallace, to believe they were his choice for
the nomination. New Dealer Jimmie Byrnes, Senator
Alben Barkley, Speaker Sam Rayburn and a host of
outside hopefuls put in a claim for the honor. But only

one man, Senator Harry S. Truman, was acceptable to all the party leaders. He was industrious, inoffensive and a party regular, qualities which rank high in the eyes of political bosses.

Jonathan Daniels, one of Truman's biographers, noting the irony in the party leaders' choice, wrote: "Truman was nominated by men speculating beyond the death of Roosevelt who knew what they wanted but did not know what they were getting."

The convention opened on July 19th and the next day Roosevelt was almost unanimously renominated. That afternoon Truman was summoned to Democratic National Chairman Robert E. Hannegan's hotel suite. There, the assembled party leaders asked the Senator to accept the vice-presidential nomination. He refused. Hannegan showed him a letter in which Roosevelt endorsed both Truman and Supreme Court Justice William O. Douglas as running mates. (The letter originally had listed Douglas's name first; Hannegan had persuaded Roosevelt to reverse the order.) Still Truman refused. Hannegan telephoned Roosevelt, whose booming voice could be heard clearly by everyone in the room.

"Bob," the President said, "have you got that fellow lined up yet?"

"No," replied Hannegan. "He is the contrariest Missouri mule I've ever dealt with."

"Well, you tell him if he wants to break up the Democratic Party in the middle of a war that's his responsibility," Roosevelt said and hung up.

Truman no longer could resist. "Well, if that is the

situation," he said, pacing the floor, "I'll have to say yes, but why the hell didn't he tell me in the first place?"

Wallace, however, refused to give up. A pre-convention poll on the nomination had shown Democratic voters favored: Wallace, 65 percent; Barkley, 17 percent; Byrnes, 3 percent; and Truman, 2 percent. "I am in this fight to the finish," Wallace told reporters. On the first ballot, with 589 votes needed for victory, Wallace outpolled Truman, 429½ to 319½. But that proved to be the limit of the Vice-President's strength. Truman won the nomination on the second ballot, in a wild, vote-switching finish, 1031 to 105.

He had come a long way. Born in 1884 in Lamar, Missouri, he had enjoyed a typical boyhood on the family farm in Grandview, 18 miles south of Kansas City. He frolicked in the cornfields, searched for birds' nests in the tall prairie grass and consumed quantities of homemade preserves and pies. "Those were wonderful days and great adventures," he later recalled.

When he was six, the family moved to Independence. Two years later Truman was fitted with glasses and sent to school. His mother already had taught him how to read, and he spent most of his time with books. "By the time I was thirteen or fourteen years old," he said, "I had read all the books in the Independence Public Library and our big old Bible three times through."

His favorite subject was history. Looking back, he saw it as "solid instruction and wise teaching which I somehow felt that I wanted and needed." And, indeed,

what he learned about Lincoln's handling of the insubordinate General George B. McClellan and about Andrew Johnson's difficulties in succeeding a great President later proved invaluable.

In 1901 Truman was graduated from high school. Unable to afford college, and barred from West Point by his poor eyesight, he took clerical jobs with the railroad, the Kansas City *Star* and two local banks. After five years in the city, he returned to Grandview to help run his grandfather's farm, and there he remained until America's entry into World War I.

Truman had joined the National Guard as a private in 1905; now he was appointed lieutenant and sent to training camp, where he ran the regimental canteen and became a crack artillery officer. His reward was an overseas assignment and command of Battery D of the 129th Field Artillery. In France he narrowly escaped death, silenced his share of German batteries, advanced to captain and celebrated the Allied victory in Paris and Nice. When he returned to Missouri, he married Bess Wallace, a childhood sweetheart.

Back in Independence, Truman opened a haberdashery with the man who had helped him run the regimental canteen so successfully. The store prospered until the recession of 1921, when the partners were forced to close the business at a loss. Truman later described this as a "hard experience" but a not uncommon one which was magnified beyond its significance by his subsequent notability.

At this time he also entered politics. He was well known and well liked locally and a natural campaigner.

With the backing of Boss Tom Pendergast's Kansas City organization, Truman was elected, in 1922, judge of the county court, an administrative job. In 1924 he ran for reelection and suffered his only political defeat. Two years later, he was elected presiding judge of Jackson County, which includes Kansas City. This, too, was an administrative job, and Truman gave the county the soundest, most honest administration it ever had known. He supervised the spending of $60 million on much-needed roads, hospitals and public buildings without a hint of graft. When Truman left the court to run for the U. S. Senate, Jackson was one of the few counties in Missouri that was financially solvent.

All this was accomplished under the endorsement of the Pendergast machine, an organization not noted for its incorruptibility. Pendergast called his protege "the contrariest man in the state of Missouri" when Truman insisted on awarding construction contracts to the lowest bidders. Nevertheless, he elected him at election time. For his part, Truman proved that you can't always tell a man by the company he keeps. As the noted Senator George W. Norris said of him: "I never knew an instance . . . that the bosses or the machine controlled his official work."

In 1934 Truman won a Senate seat. His first act was to call on the President "to tell him that I had been elected on his platform of 1932 and that I expected to support him." He kept the pledge. And, working hard and saying little, he gained the respect of his fellow Senators. But in 1940 he had to scramble through a three-way Democratic primary (which in

Missouri was tantamount to election) for a second term. Tom Pendergast had been imprisoned for failing to report as taxable income a $315,000 bribe, and Truman was attacked for his association with him. "When Tom Pendergast was down and out, a convicted man, people wanted me to denounce him," Truman said. "I refused. . . . I wouldn't kick a friend."

Instead he campaigned widely and persuaded Robert E. Hannegan, at that time St. Louis's Democratic boss, to support him in St. Louis in exchange for support in Kansas City for Hannegan's gubernatorial candidate. With Hannegan's organization, the remains of Pendergast's machine and the aging veterans of Battery D, Truman won the primary by a slender margin.

He returned to Washington and persuaded the Senate to form a Special Committee to Investigate the National Defense Program, which was just getting underway. Truman wanted to avoid the bottlenecks, waste and graft that traditionally characterize the letting of government defense contracts. "Public contractors," he said, "are not very good spenders of public money unless watched."

The committee, which was headed by Truman, functioned brilliantly. On a total appropriation of $400,000, it saved the nation $15 *billion*. Truman became a power in the Senate and a prospect for national office. Early in 1944, Washington correspondents voted him the civilian who, next to Roosevelt, knew most about the war. That summer he was nominated for the vice-presidency, and in November he was elected on the Roosevelt ticket. So ended his Senate career—

"the happiest ten years of my life"—and began what he later would call "the year of decision."

Roosevelt's fourth term began under overcast skies and ended, 82 days later, with his fatal stroke in Warm Springs, Georgia. When news of the President's death reached Mrs. Roosevelt, Truman was summoned to the White House. He thought Roosevelt had returned early from his vacation in Warm Springs and wanted to confer with him. Instead he was ushered into Mrs. Roosevelt's study, where she, her daughter, her son-in-law and the White House press secretary awaited him. Mrs. Roosevelt stepped forward and laid her arm on Truman's shoulder.

"Harry," she said quietly, "the President is dead."

Truman was stunned. Although he had known that Roosevelt was weary and spent, he was unprepared for his death. He had not allowed himself to think about it. Now, for a moment, he could not bring himself to speak. When, at last, he found his voice, he asked Mrs. Roosevelt:

"Is there anything I can do for you?"

"Is there anything *we* can do for *you?*" she replied. "For you are the one in trouble now."

Shortly afterwards, Harry S. Truman took the oath of office as the 33rd President of the United States. Only a few hours before, he had been presiding over the Senate while that body debated the Mexican Treaty on water in the Colorado River and the Rio Grande. Now, in one stroke, he had inherited the problems of the entire nation and of most of Europe and Asia as well. "Boys," he told reporters the next day, peering through the thick-lensed glasses he wore, "if you ever pray, pray for me now. . . . I've got the most terribly responsible job a man ever had."

His training for it had been minimal. Although he had been an administrator in Jackson County and a legislator in the Senate, neither experience could be said to have prepared him for the awesome responsibilities which now were his. "Within the first few months," Truman wrote later, "I discovered that being a President is like riding a tiger. A man has to keep on riding or be swallowed. . . . I never felt that I could let up for a single moment."

The vice-presidency had been no help either, despite Roosevelt's expansion of the office. "It is a mighty leap from the vice-presidency to the presidency," Truman said later, "when one is forced to make it without warning." With the nation at war, Truman's difficulties were compounded. He had not even been told about the atomic bomb.

Perhaps no President, accidental or elected, ever faced more momentous challenges than Truman did in his seven years in office. The use of the atomic bomb, European recovery, the Berlin blockade, the Korean War and how to meet China's intervention in that war were just a few of the explosive issues that demanded presidential action.

His initial reaction to his succession was to plead his "unfitness" and "inadequacy" for the presidency. When some of these comments were reported in the newspapers, Senator Barkley, an old friend, went to see Truman. "Have confidence in yourself," he advised the President. "If you do not, the people will lose confidence in you. However humble and contrite you feel, you have got to go forward and lead this nation out of war."

He not only led the nation out of war but into a new age, the age of the atom. The first atomic device was exploded in the New Mexico desert on July 16, 1945. Ten days later the Potsdam Declaration called upon the Japanese to surrender unconditionally or face "prompt and utter destruction." The Japanese rejected the ultimatum, and on August 6th an atom bomb was dropped on Hiroshima, virtually destroying that city. "We have spent $2 billion on the greatest scientific gamble in history—and won," Truman announced. The bombing prompted the Russians, who had been vacillating, to declare war against Japan (so as to share in the spoils), but the Japanese still held out. On August 9th a second bomb devastated Nagasaki. The next day the Japanese government announced its willingness to surrender.

Was the use of the bomb necessary? That question still haunts many Americans. The Japanese government had indicated its willingness to negotiate peace, but it had balked at accepting "unconditional surrender." It sought assurance that the Emperor would remain sovereign. The Potsdam Declaration, however, deliberately omitted mention of the Emperor, and when the Japanese rejected the Declaration, the choice seemed to lie between invading Japan and dropping the bomb. American estimates of casualties in an invasion ran from 250,000 to 1,000,000 men. Naturally, the government wished to avoid these if it could. It also wished to end the war before Russia got into it to preclude giving the Russians, who were proving intractable in Europe, a voice in the Asian settlement.

Truman's special advisory committee on the bomb (which included eminent educators and scientists as well as government and military officials) concluded that dropping the bomb on a target city was preferable to invasion. A technical demonstration of the power of the bomb was ruled out as unpredictable and psychologically unsound.

"From what I know today," said the project's chief scientist, J. Robert Oppenheimer, 20 years later, "I do not believe that we could have known with any degree of certainty that the atomic bomb was necessary to end the war. But that was not the view of those who had studied the situation at the time and who were thinking of an invasion of Japan. Probably they were wrong."

Historian Samuel Eliot Morison doesn't think so. Even after the two atomic bombs had been dropped and the sovereignty of the Emperor had been assured, he says, "surrender was a very near thing." The Emperor had to override his two chief military advisers. And even then, "a military coup d'etat to sequester the Emperor, kill his Cabinet and continue the war was narrowly averted."

Truman never questioned his decision. "Let there be no mistake about it," he later wrote. "I regarded the bomb as a military weapon and never had any doubt that it should be used."

But Gar Alperovitz, a political economist who recently made a detailed study of the political impact of the bomb, concludes that "presently available evidence shows the atomic bomb was not needed to end the war or to save lives—and that this was understood by American leaders at the time. . . . Before the bomb was dropped," he adds, "each of the Joint Chiefs of Staff advised that it was highly likely that Japan could be forced to surrender 'unconditionally' without use of the bomb and without an invasion."

Alperovitz suggests that the bomb was used as a threat, a symbol of power, a lever in the already-dawning worldwide political struggle between East and West.

Certainly the pressures for using the bomb were "tremendous," Hanson W. Baldwin, the distinguished military analyst, has noted. "Huge amounts had been spent on it; a vast machinery was dedicated solely to its development and employment." How much control Truman actually had over it is debatable. The bomb was perhaps the first of those scientific-military enterprises which, inflated by billions of dollars, develop a life and momentum of their own and defy the control of any individual.

After the war, Truman's problems continued unabated. Postwar inflation and labor-management strife sowed domestic discontent, and the "cold war" of power politics between Russia and her former allies stirred international uneasiness.

In the last quarter of 1945 Truman unveiled his "Fair Deal": legislative proposals for full and fair employment, housing subsidies, health insurance, free medical care, aid to education, nationalization of atomic energy, and development of the St. Lawrence Seaway. Little of it was enacted by Congress, which in 1946 fell under Republican control for the first time in 14 years. By then, both parties had come to view Truman as a caretaker President.

Truman remained undaunted. In 1948, an election year, he guided the Marshall Plan, a generous program to aid European economic recovery, through the quicksands of a conservative Congress. "For any President at any time this would have been a great accomplishment," says historian Richard E. Neustadt. At this time, in Truman's situation, it was "almost miraculous."

As the Marshall Plan became law, the Russians posed the first direct confrontation with the United States by arbitrarily blockading the land and water approaches to Berlin, which lay deep inside the Russian occupation zone. This left Truman with several alternatives. One was to submit to Russian conditions for lifting the blockade. Another was to abandon Berlin. A third was to challenge the roadblocks. And a fourth was to circumvent them. The first two assured political defeat; the last two risked an incident that might trigger armed conflict.

Truman, determined to maintain American presence in the German capital with the minimum risk of war, responded with the Berlin airlift. Food, fuel and other supplies were flown into Berlin via the air corridor which all the occupying powers shared. International tension increased. But no incident occurred, and after

321 days, the Russians lifted the blockade as suddenly as they had lowered it. Truman later said that the Russians "truculence" in the Berlin blockade was a key factor in the formation of the North Atlantic Treaty Organization.

Meanwhile, at home, Truman was plagued by inflation, petty Administration scandals and legislative rebuffs in Congress. As the 1948 elections approached, he was written off as a too-little man in a too-big job, and Thomas E. Dewey, the youthful Governor of New York who had lost to Roosevelt in 1944, confidently prepared to move into the White House. With the popular Governor of California, Earl Warren, also on the ticket, the Republicans appeared unbeatable.

Truman's own party split into three factions. The regulars, after failing to persuade General Dwight D. Eisenhower to run, reluctantly nominated Truman. (Truman, unable to get Justice William O. Douglas as his running mate, settled for seventy-year-old Senator Alben W. Barkley.) Distressed over Truman's commitment to civil rights, southern "Dixiecrats" named their own candidate, South Carolina's Governor J. Strom Thurmond. And disgruntled radicals nominated Henry Wallace to run under the banner of the Progressive Party.

The public opinion polls showed Truman losing badly, the politicians conceded his defeat and the press heralded it. But the game President refused to quit. He called a special session of the Republican-controlled Congress and dared the Republicans to legislate the programs on inflation, housing, education and civil rights "which they are saying they are for in their platform." None of the programs was enacted. Truman then made an extended whistle-stop tour of the nation excoriating the "do-nothing" Republican Congress. It proved effective. In the most stunning upset in presidential politics, Truman won the election despite the loss of four southern states to Thurmond. The margin in popular votes was better than 2 million; in the electoral college it was 303 to 189. Truman was President in his own right.

One of his first acts was to obtain legislation designating the Vice-President as a member of the powerful National Security Council. Established under Truman in 1947, the Council deals with "the integration of domestic, foreign and military policies relating to national security." The Act which created it, said Truman, "represented one of the outstanding achievements of my Administration." And it marked the most significant upgrading of the vice-presidency up to that time. Never again would a Vice-President be kept ignorant of a vital project like the atomic bomb.

It was in his first full term that Truman met his greatest challenge—Korea. He called it "the toughest decision I had to make as President."

The Korean peninsula had been partitioned along the 38th parallel into North and South zones by the wartime allies pending resolution of Korea's political future. By 1958 separate North and South Korean governments had emerged, one under Russian and the other under American hegemony. Then, in June, 1950, North Korean forces equipped with Soviet-supplied weapons invaded South Korea. The United Nations (prodded by the American delegation) condemned the attack, and the world, East and West, waited for the American response. "The time has come," one European diplomat cabled his government from Washington, "when Uncle Sam must put up or shut up, and my guess is he will do neither."

But Truman, determined to "contain" Soviet-inspired aggression, ordered American air and naval units to support the beleaguered South Koreans. And the same day the United Nations adopted a United States resolution calling upon UN members to "furnish such assistance to the Republic of Korea as may be necessary to repel the armed attack and to restore international peace and security in the area." This cloaked American action with United Nations sanction. "The President," declared the New York *Herald Tribune,* expressing the predominent national sentiment, "has acted—and spoken—with a magnificent courage and terse decision."

A few days later, Truman named General Douglas MacArthur, the wartime hero of the Pacific, Commander of the United Nations forces. MacArthur halted the swift North Korean advance and, in a brilliant counteroffensive, pushed the invaders back across the 38th parallel and north almost to the Yalu River at the Chinese border. The sweep north, however, went beyond the policy of containment and provoked China to enter the conflict. Hordes of Chinese "volunteers" now poured across the Yalu and turned the tide of battle.

Truman was faced with a new problem. "There was no doubt that we had reached a point where grave decisions had to be made," he said. "If we chose to extend the war to China . . . we had to anticipate Russian intervention."

MacArthur wanted to bomb China and the bridges over the Yalu. Truman forbade it. "Every decision I made in connection with the Korean conflict," he said later, "had this one aim in mind: to prevent a third world war and the terrible destruction it would bring to the civilized world." But MacArthur, in defiance of the President's policy, released a statement obliquely threatening China with air and naval attack. Truman viewed this as "a challenge to the authority of the President under the Constitution" and relieved the General of his command for insubordination. It was an unpopular decision but it preserved the constitutional principle of civilian control of the military.

Meanwhile, the battle line shifted back to the vicinity of the 38th parallel and there became stabilized. Truce negotiations opened in July, 1951, dragged on for two years and finally ended in a cease-fire which fixed a demilitarized boundary between the two countries along a line roughly equivalent to the 38th parallel. The actual cease-fire was agreed upon by Truman's successor, Dwight D. Eisenhower. Truman, deciding not to run for reelection in 1952, returned to private life in Independence, Missouri.

Truman's stature has increased with the passage of time. The social and humanistic programs he advocated in 1945 since have been enacted. Control of atomic energy remains where he placed it—in civilian hands. And his limitation of the Korean War has proved statesmanlike, especially in view of the tragedy in Vietnam.

He was controversial and often inconsistent. "At times," says historian Clinton Rossiter, "he had the look of greatness, at times he gave off the sound of meanness." But always he was a strong President. The presidency, he once said, was "where the buck stopped." His job, as he saw it, was to make decisions and to take the initiative. "The President's got to set the sights," he said. And that is what he did.

This is a sad time for all people.

—LYNDON B. JOHNSON in his first public statement as President

8 Lyndon B. Johnson: 1963

Lyndon Johnson, who had flown into Dallas in *Air Force Two,* left that fateful city a few hours later in *Air Force One* with the body of his slain predecessor in a rear compartment. The transition from number two to number one, in all respects, had been sudden, swift and total.

By 6 P.M. he was back in Washington. At the airport, he told a stunned nation: "This is a sad time for all people. . . . I will do my best. That is all I can do. I ask for your help and God's." Then, with three of the late President's advisers, he shuttled by helicopter to the White House to prepare the course of his own presidency.

It was to be one of continuity. Johnson saw that his first task was to secure the public's confidence in his leadership and in the government's stability in the wake of violence. He did this by stressing the uninterrupted flow of leadership in the government. First, he persuaded the Cabinet and presidential advisers to stay on. Then, five days after the assassination, he addressed a joint session of Congress and an anxious nation. Quoting John F. Kennedy's inaugural exhortation, "Let us begin . . ." the new President paused, then added, "Today, in this moment of new resolve, I would say to all my fellow Americans, let us continue."

The nation was reassured by Johnson's words, by his manner, by his presence. Theodore H. White, Pulitzer Prize-winning historian, called the President's performance "superb." And well it might be, for Johnson was playing a part for which he long had prepared himself. Even Kennedy in 1960 had admitted, "If I didn't want this job myself, I'd get behind Lyndon. He's the ablest man I know in American politics and he really cares about this country as I want a President to care." And, after the assassination, one Washington observer had noted about Johnson: "It almost seems as though he was fated to be President. This man *needed* to be President—it's the only office big enough for him."

The 36th President of the United States was born in 1908 in a modest frame house on the banks of the Pedernales River near Johnson City, Texas, which had been named after his grandfather. His mother was a former teacher of elocution, and his father was a politician, onetime teacher and dabbler in real estate. An easygoing man, the elder Johnson was seldom solvent. But that was the common lot in that part of Texas.

Johnson's Texas is not the Texas of rich oil fields, blooming cotton lands or lush prairies. It is hard hill country, a bleak land of stunted trees and dusty soil, drought and flash floods. In this harsh environment, a man must scrabble for a living, and the struggle leaves its mark on most. Texas hill country men are notable more for hard trading and relentless drive than for sensitivity and compassion.

Lyndon Johnson began life in deprivation determined not to end it that way. About his childhood little is known, if the budding legends are discounted. When Johnson was five years old, the family moved to Johnson City. His mother had taught him the alphabet at age three, and in school he was a bright, eager student.

He was graduated from high school at age fifteen. In a class of six he was president and debating champion. His mother wanted him to go to college, but Johnson instead drove to California in a battered Model T with five friends in search of fortune. "We were like something right out of *The Grapes of Wrath,*" one of the adventurers recalls. "What little stake we had we buried in the ground at night."

They found not fortune but menial jobs as waiters, dishwashers and fruit pickers, and after a few months of this Johnson hitchhiked back home. Again spurning his mother's pleas to try college, he went to work on a road gang for two years.

By 1927 he had had enough of pushing a wheelbarrow. Borrowing $75, he enrolled at Southwest Texas State Teacher's College in nearby San Marcos.

There he showed the political style and personal drive that were to mark his career. Student affairs at State were run by an entrenched group of athletes known as the "Black Stars." Johnson tried to join them, but he failed to make the baseball team and was rebuffed. So he organized a rival group, the "White Stars," and in his first election scored an upset by persuading the "independents" to vote with his White Stars against the athletes. "He was after everybody," a former classmate recalls. "If he was in a café, he'd make it a point to let everybody know who he was and get everybody's name, and he never forgot anything."

To help pay his tuition, he worked, beginning as a janitor and gardener at State. Within a month he had talked his way into a job as secretary to the president. Years later, Johnson's former boss told him, "I could hardly tell who was president—you or me."

Johnson majored in history in college but undoubtedly got more out of extracurricular activities than out of any classroom. In 1930 he was graduated, and he took a job teaching speech and coaching debaters at a high school in Houston. A year later, when Richard M. Kleberg, the head of Texas's largest spread, the fabulous King Ranch, ran for an unexpired term in Congress, Johnson worked hard in his campaign. Kleberg won and took the bright, energetic young teacher with him to Washington as his secretary.

So began Johnson's political career, in the gloom of the Great Depression. As always, he worked hard at his job. Under the tutelage of two shrewd Texans, Sam Rayburn and John Nance Garner, Johnson learned the intricacies of cloakroom politics—the hard bartering that oils the democratic legislative process. He was a willing and able pupil.

In 1934 he married Claudia Alta ("Lady Bird") Taylor of Austin, Texas, after a brief courtship which was conducted mostly by telephone and telegram between Washington and Austin. "It was all typical of Lyndon," says a friend. "I'm sure he saw her, made up his mind he wanted to marry her and did."

Mrs. Johnson proved to be as astute as she was gracious, especially in business and politics. Some observers credit the burgeoning of the Johnson personal fortune, which is valued from $4 to $14 million, to her management.

Johnson attended law school at night for a semester in 1935. But he gave this up when President Roosevelt, at the request of Congressman Rayburn, appointed him Director of the National Youth Administration in Texas. The NYA, one of the host of new agencies and programs of the New Deal, was designed to provide work or schooling for the five million youngsters made idle by the Depression. Johnson did a spectacular job salvaging youths and in the process built a personal political following. When, in 1937, the Congressman from Johnson's district died, the young administrator filed to fill the unexpired term. He won easily, running as a confirmed New Dealer. After the victory, President Roosevelt interrupted a vacation cruise to meet Johnson in Galveston. Roosevelt liked the lanky, ingratiating Texan and later opened the lines of power to him. To intimates the President confided that Johnson was the kind of young man he might have been, if he had not been saddled with a Harvard education.

The new Congressman served his constituents well. Acting on the principle that there is something for everyone, and you get yours and I get mine, Johnson obtained more public projects and more federal money for his district than any man in Congress. He was re-elected to the House three times. But the Senate was his goal, and in 1941, when Texas Senator Morris Sheppard died, Johnson ran to fill his unexpired term. Campaigning again as a New Dealer, he lost to folksy, flamboyant Governor W. Lee ("Pappy") O'Daniel, a guitar-strumming former flour salesman. Johnson actually led by 5,000 votes when the polls closed, but late, "corrected" returns from rural counties gave O'Daniel a 1,311 margin. The defeat was a lesson to Johnson in political arithmetic—and in the waning popularity of the New Deal in Texas.

He went back to the House. During the war, he served a seven-month stint overseas as a naval reserve officer and headed a subcommittee investigating naval procurement methods. In 1948, he again ran for the Senate, this time on a conservative, segregationist platform. Johnson is, above all, a politician, and the first law of politics is to get elected. He saw which way the wind was blowing and he blew with it. But his rival, Governor Coke Stevenson, was even more conservative, and better known, and he appeared to have won the primary by 113 votes when he was counted out by late-late returns from a border hamlet which gave Johnson victory by 87 votes. His arithmetic clearly improved, Johnson easily defeated his Republican opponent in November and went on to the Senate, where he was dubbed "Landslide Lyndon."

The United States Senate resembles nothing so much as a combination private club and brokerage house. Its base is privilege, its commodity is power; and, as always, the first derives from the second. In such a body, Johnson was bound to flourish, for he is a born trader with an instinct for power. "He knows exactly how far you will go to get what you want," says one observer. "He believes men are moved by influence, not argument."

His first move was to ingratiate himself with the conservative Richard Russell of Georgia, perhaps the most prestigious of the Senate's powerful "inner circle." With Russell's blessing, Johnson in 1950 became the Democratic Whip, whose job it is to round up Senators when their votes are needed. In 1952, a Republican year, he became the Minority Leader. And, when the Democrats regained control of the Senate in 1954, Johnson, having been reelected handily, became Majority Leader.

As Senate Leader, Johnson mobilized the feuding elements of the Democratic Party for legislative action. North and South, conservative and radical, rich and poor—he forged all of these into a Democratic voting bloc through astute *quid pro quo* trades, a select distribution of desirable committee assignments and personal privileges and the force of his own personality. He cultivated the Republicans, too. Garner once told him, "You'll need friends on both sides of the aisle," and Johnson never forgot that.

Nothing was left to chance. His staff researched the

practical chances of every bill: who would support it, who would oppose it, who was open to persuasion. The idea was to accomplish the possible through diligent preparation. If persuasion was necessary, Johnson applied what became known as "The Treatment." Its tone, reported Washington correspondents Rowland Evans and Robert Novak, "could be supplication, accusation, cajolery, exuberance, scorn, tears, complaint, the hint of threat." Johnson delivered this monologue rapid-fire, nose-to-nose, anticipating objectives and underlining his arguments with clippings and statistics which he plucked from his pocket. "Mimicry, humor, and a genius for analogy made The Treatment an almost hypnotic experience," concluded Evans and Novak, "and rendered the target stunned and helpless."

Johnson's reign in the Senate continued, interrupted only by a "moderately severe" heart attack in 1955, until 1960 when he sought the Democratic nomination for President. Sharing his ambition were Senators Stuart Symington of Missouri, Hubert Humphrey of Minnesota and John F. Kennedy of Massachusetts. Adlai Stevenson, a two-time loser to Dwight D. Eisenhower, waited in the wings for the call to duty. Kennedy, however, in a well-financed, brilliantly coordinated campaign, crushed Humphrey in the primaries and garnered enough delegate strength to win the nomination on the first ballot. The deadlock for which Johnson and Symington had waited never developed. Stevenson's call never came.

In a surprise move, Kennedy offered the vice-presidential nomination to Johnson. Accounts of the details of the proposal differ, but it seems clear that expediency dictated the choice. Kennedy thought Johnson a highly qualified candidate, but, more important, he needed him on the ticket to win southern votes.

Speaker Sam Rayburn at first advised Johnson against accepting. And another Johnson mentor, John Nance Garner, told him, "The vice-presidency isn't worth a pitcher of warm spit!" But Johnson himself was eager to run. The vice-presidency would make him a national rather than a sectional politician, and he would be only sixty years old when Kennedy's second term ended. To a friend who warned him not to exchange the power of Senate Majority Leader for the shell of the vice-presidency, Johnson replied, "Power is where power goes." He thought it would go with him to the presiding chair of the Senate.

Johnson's presence on the ticket carried the South in what was the closest election in almost a century. The Vice-President now tried to exercise the power he was sure he had brought with him. But he discovered that he wielded a paper sword. The Senate rebuffed his attempt to control it from the chair; the President ignored his unprecedented bid for "general supervision" over areas normally reserved for the Chief Executive; even his wishes on patronage were disregarded.

Kennedy did make him Chairman of the National Aeronautics and Space Council and of the President's Committee on Equal Employment Opportunity. And he included him in White House policy-making conferences. But Johnson was ill at ease in the "New Frontier." His gritty, expansive, populist style was alien—and outdated—to the young eastern intellectuals and urban sophisticates who formed the bulk of the Kennedy Administration. So, in the words of one observer, Johnson remained "emotionally detached" from the presidential team. And, in the area of congressional relations, where he might have helped push the President's stalled legislative proposals, he did nothing. "Johnson," said one of his aides, "sat on the sidelines. He thought they were messing it up in congress. He was like an old coach watching the boys play and nobody let him explain the game."

Then suddenly, in Dallas, the game, the team, the players became his. And, after the first flash of sympathy for the new President, the American people waited to see what he would do.

There was plenty to do. Throughout the nation, the Negro was increasingly pressing for his civil rights; in the cities, the quality of life was rapidly deteriorating; abroad, a minor skirmish in Vietnam was escalating into a major American war. There were many other challenges, but these were the ones that would measure Lyndon Johnson's presidency.

The first obstacle was Congress. Ambrose Bierce, the nineteenth-century American satirist, once described Congress as "a body of men who meet to repeal laws." By the 1960's this could be shortened to: "a body of men who meet." Congress was doing little, and taking a long time to do that. The promises of the new Frontier—in civil rights, in education, in medical care, in housing, in tax reform—were gathering dust in the pigeonholes of hostile committees.

Kennedy had submitted to Congress a bill outlawing segregation in hotels, restaurants and other such facilities. The strongest civil rights bill since Reconstruction days, it was expected to be killed by a Senate filibuster. Could Johnson save it? More important, how hard would he try? For 20 years, as a Congressman and as a Senator, he had consistently voted against such legislation. Not until 1957 had he supported a civil rights bill—and then only after weakening it enough to please Georgia's Senator Richard Russell.

Johnson was not himself a militant segregationist; that seems clear. A more likely explanation of his record is that, as a representative of Texas, he was reflecting the wishes of his constituents. But, whatever he may have been, he now saw himself as "President of all the people," and he realized that civil rights had become a popular cause. So, applying the moral force of his office and the persuasive tactics of his Senate days, he pried the bill out of committee. Then, working behind the scenes, he helped shut off the predictable filibuster, 71 to 29—the first time such a filibuster had been broken. A few days later, the Civil Rights Act of 1964, stripping away the galling *white only* signs from public accommodations, was voted into law.

It was a remarkable display of executive direction. There was a fitting irony involved, too. Lyndon Johnson had pushed through legislation which, nearly a century ago, his namesake, Andrew Johnson, had resisted bitterly.

Not surprisingly, Johnson's two major challenges—civil rights and Vietnam—became campaign issues in

1964. Senator Barry Goldwater of Arizona, the Republican candidate for President, had voted steadfastly against the Civil Rights Act. Now he campaigned against what he called "crime in the streets" and for "carrying the war to North Vietnam." Johnson eagerly picked up the challenge. He promised moderation abroad, responsibility at home and the Great Society for everyone. By comparison Goldwater was made to appear a militant, reckless extremist, and his own speeches served to confirm this impression. Johnson, sensing victory, campaigned vigorously to increase its margin.

He had assured his own nomination in the spring with his brilliant performance in the presidency. The only suspense had been over his choice of running mate. This had turned into a protracted game of cat-and-mouse, for Johnson is compulsively secretive about his every intention. Finally, he had anointed the Senate Majority Leader from Minnesota, Hubert H. Humphrey, after extracting from him a pledge of absolute loyalty and subservience.

With his own experience to guide him, Johnson appears to have chosen Humphrey for his presidential potential. At least no element of expediency was obvious, perhaps because Goldwater's impossible candidacy had made expediency unnecessary.

The nation, offered by Goldwater "a choice, not an echo," chose a moderate Lyndon Johnson by a landslide. Johnson won all but 5 states, and his margin in the popular vote was more than 15 million. The Johnson landslide also swept into Congress many new, young Democrats who ordinarily would have lost to established Republicans. With this extra margin, the President decided to ram his Great Society programs through Congress while his mandate was still impressive. He told his legislative aides:

"I was just elected President by the biggest popular margin in the history of the country, fifteen million votes. Just by the natural way people think, and because Barry Goldwater scared hell out of them, I have already lost about two of these fifteen and am probably getting down to thirteen. If I get in any fight with Congress, I will lose another couple of million. And if I have to send any more of our boys into Vietnam, I may be down to eight million by the end of the summer."

His appraisal proved accurate. The consensus he had built cracked in the fall. But by then he had pushed through Congress the long-delayed Medicare bill, major antipoverty and housing legislation, federal aid to education, water pollution controls and a civil rights bill outlawing discrimination at the polls. Not since Franklin Roosevelt's first 100 days had such a torrent of social legislation been enacted. A New York *Times* correspondent, expressing the general assessment of Johnson's own first 100 days, noted that they "may rank as one of the most remarkable periods of domestic achievement in American history."

In Vietnam, however, the situation had festered, and Johnson was forced to focus virtually all his attention on a "dirty little war" 10,000 miles away.

Everything about this war has been controversial. There has been disagreement over its nature, over its purpose, over the United States commitment to it, over American use of power and diplomacy. Only its impact is indisputable. It has caused the death and disfigurations of millions; decimated Vietnam; consumed uncounted billions of dollars; distorted American foreign policy; alienated world opinion; mesmerized the Administration; and divided and confused the American people.

It is impossible, in this space, to write about Vietnam comprehensively. It is difficult even to assess Johnson's role in Vietnam. More information and years, perhaps decades, of perspective will be needed to evaluate it. Yet, unquestionably, Vietnam was Johnson's greatest challenge, perhaps even his Waterloo. So, an attempt must be made to determine how he responded to this challenge.

Johnson characterized the war as "aggression" by the North Vietnamese which the United States is resisting to preserve the "freedom" of the South Vietnamese. This may be dismissed as rhetoric for public consumption. The realities, whatever they may be, are not so uncomplicated. Impartial evidence, in fact, indicates that the American-supported Saigon regime touched off the conflict in 1956 by suppressing in South Vietnam the free elections which had been promised under the Geneva Agreement of 1954. And a long succession of corrupt dictatorial Saigon juntas can hardly be said to have watered the seeds of Vietnamese freedom.

More important than the reason behind American involvement in Vietnam is the question of the extension of American power in Asia. Theodore Roosevelt once said: "I never take a step in foreign policy unless I am assured that I shall be able eventually to carry out my will by force." Perhaps thinking along those lines, Eisenhower pledged aid to Saigon but kept it limited; Kennedy sent a few thousand military "advisers" to Vietnam. Johnson, campaigning in 1964, counseled continued restraint. "We don't want our American boys to do the fighting for Asian boys," he said. But in February, 1965, he ordered daily air attacks on North Vietnam; and by 1968 more than 500,000 American combat troops had assumed the burden of fighting in South Vietnam.

Was it worth it? Americans asked themselves. The commitment of all those men and resources brought only more death and suffering to both sides in Vietnam, while in America the cities continued to decay, poverty and racial unrest increased and the ability of democracy itself to meet the challenges of the Sixties was being questioned.

Even the people's faith in the government suffered. The difference between what the Administration said and what it did grew wider as the war escalated, creating a "credibility gap" which Walter Lippman called "the result of a deliberate policy of artificial manipulation of official news. The purpose of this manipulation," Lippman added, "is to create a consensus for the President, to stifle debate about his aims and his policies, to thwart deep probing into what has already happened, what is actually happening, what is going to happen."

Lyndon Johnson began his presidency hoping "to unite the American people." He failed to do that, and on March 31, 1968, recognizing the "divisiveness among us all," he removed himself from consideration for renomination to a second full term. Within weeks preliminary peace talks were opened in Paris with the North Vietnamese.

Despite his larger failure, Johnson probably will rank high among American Presidents for his domestic legislative achievements. He was, in the words of political analyst Tom Wicker, "an indefatigable doer, a man of power and pride and action who pushed hard for what he wanted, achieved much of it and broke a lot of traditions and taboos in the process.

"It was said of him," Wicker adds, "that he wanted to be loved, and often acted like it, but in the long run he usually gave action a higher priority than affection. As a result, he got more of the former than the latter."

Epilogue

The last third of the twentieth century has begun with the promise of further revolutionary change throughout the world. What will America's role be in it? In the first third of the century, America, under Theodore Roosevelt, became a world power. In the second third, under another Vice-President of destiny, Harry Truman, the United States assumed leadership of the West. Will it now use this power to help redress the chronic imbalance between rich and poor, strong and weak, white and nonwhite, industrial and agrarian? Will it apply its vast human and material resources to the urgent problems of arms control, food production, population explosion and urban development? Or will it succumb to what Senator J. W. Fulbright of Mississippi has called that "arrogance of power" in which a nation, driven by an inflated sense of its own infallibility, piously attempts to shape the world in its own image?

Which way will America move? The direction may determine the quality of life for the next several decades. And that direction will be set by the man elected to the White House—or by his running mate suddenly elevated to power. The next Vice-President of destiny is somewhere among us. He may already be serving.

Bibliographical Note

This is not intended to be an exhaustive list of the books, manuscripts, letters and periodicals which I consulted for this study. Rather than cite a long list of source materials which are not readily accessible to the general reader, I shall note below what I consider the one or two outstanding books on each of my subjects so that any reader who wishes to delve more deeply into that subject may do so with pleasure as well as with profit.

There are many informative books about the presidency, but the most cogent and stimulating is Richard E. Neustadt, *Presidential Power* (New York, 1960). Another provocative study of this institution is Rexford G. Tugwell, *The Enlargement of the Presidency* (New York, 1960). Less has been written about the vice-presidency. Indeed, I found only two books of note: Irving G. Williams, *The Rise of the Vice Presidency* (Washington, 1956) and Donald Young, *American Roulette* (New York, 1965).

Of the first four Vice-Presidents of destiny, only one, Andrew Johnson, has been written about extensively. Nevertheless, each man has at least one able chronicler. Robert Seager II, *And Tyler Too* (New York, 1963) is a well-written balanced biography of John Tyler (and of his second wife, Julia). Robert J. Rayback, *Millard Fillmore* (Buffalo, 1959) is an uncritical but detailed biography of the 13th President. One of the more objective

186

and better written of the many studies of Andrew Johnson is Milton Lomask, *Andrew Johnson, President on Trial* (New York, 1960). And Kenneth M. Stampp, *The Era of Reconstruction: 1865–1877* (New York, 1965) is an important, revealing book on this period. Interesting, too, is George Frederick Howe's incisive study of machine politics, *Chester A. Arthur* (New York, 1935).

The twentieth-century Vice-Presidents of destiny have been the subject of innumerable books, including those written by three of the men themselves. George E. Mowry, *The Era of Theodore Roosevelt: 1900–1912** (New York, 1958) is an excellent, realistic study of the man and the period. More detailed, but also objective, is Henry F. Pringle's definitive biography, *Theodore Roosevelt** (New York, 1931). Either of these books is more reliable than Roosevelt's own *Autobiography* (New York, 1913), which is exhilarating but fanciful. Calvin Coolidge's *Autobiography* (New York, 1929), on the other hand, is just the opposite: pedestrian and mundane; a more penetrating study of Coolidge is William Allen White, *A Puritan in Babylon* (New York, 1938). The most candid of the presidential memoirs are Harry S. Truman, *Year of Decision** (New York, 1955) and *Years of Trial and Hope** (New York, 1956). A more objective book on this period is Cabell Phillips, *The Truman Presidency* (New York, 1966); and a most provocative one is Gar Alperovitz, *Atomic Diplomacy* (New York, 1965). Two books on Lyndon B. Johnson which are neither idolatrous nor vituperative are Michael Davie, *LBJ: A Foreign Observer's Viewpoint* (New York, 1966), and Roland Evans and Robert Novak, *The Exercise of Power* (New York, 1966). The first captures the essence of the man and the second dissects his method of operation.

Index

189

191

About the Author

JOSEPH A. ALVAREZ is a writer and editor in New York, where he was born and graduated from City College. He lives in Greenwich Village with his wife, their young daughter, two cats, and two fish. *Vice-Presidents of Destiny* is his first book published with Putnam's.

47

J920
A
Alvarez
Vice-Presidents of destiny